PATHWAYS
TO

BY SCOTT ALLAN

MASTERY
THE SERIES

scottallan@scottallanpublishing.com

Empower Your Mornings

Wake Up Early, Strengthen Your Focus, and Maximize the Quality of Your Life with a Dynamic Morning Routine

More Bestselling Titles From Scott Allan

Empower Your Thoughts

Empower Your Deep Focus

Rejection Reset

Relaunch Your Life

Drive Your Destiny

The Discipline of Masters

Do the Hard Things First

Undefeated

No Punches Pulled

Fail Big

Built for Stealth

JOIN THE COMMUNITY OF 30,000 LIFETIME LEARNERS!

Sign up today for my **free weekly newsletter** and receive instant access to **the <u>onboarding subscriber pack</u>** that includes:

The Fearless Confidence Action Guide: 9 action plans for building limitless confidence and achieving sustainable results!

The Bestseller Poster Pack: A poster set of Scott Allan's bestselling books

The Zero Procrastination Blueprint: A step-by-step blueprint to turn procrastination into rapid action implementation!

Click Here to <u>Subscribe Today</u>, or scan the <u>QR code</u>.

Empower Your
Mornings

Wake Up Early, Strengthen Your Focus, and Maximize the Quality of Your Life with a Dynamic Morning Routine

By Scott Allan

Scott Allan PUBLISHING

MASTER YOUR LIFE **ONE BOOK AT A TIME**

Contents

Introduction: Empower Your Mornings........................2

Chapter 1 :The (Unexpected) Power of

Early Rising..8

Chapter 2: Benefits of a Morning Routine..................21

Chapter 3: The Neuroscience Approach

to Morning Rituals 42

Chapter 4: The Mindset and Early Morning Routines of

Highly Successful Performers 49

Chapter 5: Building Your Evening Ritual 61

Chapter 6: How to Create Amazing Mornings.............76

Chapter 7: Building Your High-Performance

Morning Routine..91

Chapter 8: The Early Morning Habit Stack 105

Chapter 9: Obstacles: Your Family, Work,

Distractions, and Everything Else 112

Conclusion: Morning Routines 124

Empower Your Thoughts (Bonus Chapter #1) 129

Scott Allan... 147

"When you arise in the morning, think of what a precious privilege it is to be alive, to breathe, to think, to enjoy, to love."

—Marcus Aurelius

Introduction: Empower Your Mornings

"Morning is an important time of day because how you spend your morning can often tell you what kind of day you will have."

— Lemony Snicket

Based on a survey by Ipsos on behalf of the Sargento cheese company, 95% of Americans dread mornings and starting the day, which they consider a form of torture.

If you tend to hit the snooze button repeatedly, you are in good company because, according to the Ipsos survey, 43% of those polled stated they despised the sound of their alarm clock, and 39% confessed to being 'slow risers.'

The remaining 5% represents those who manage to wake up on time—a large majority without depending on an alarm clock—have a consistent morning ritual, eat a healthy breakfast, and usually begin their day on a high note.

In short, this minority group experiences empowered mornings where, instead of dreading the beginning of their day, they look forward to hopping out of bed to face it. In a nutshell, this is what empowering your mornings can help you achieve—a purposeful, positive, energized, and fresh outlook toward the day ahead.

This begs a few questions:

- *How can you go about empowering your mornings?*

- *Which habits can you adopt to help in your pursuit to begin your day on the right footing?*

- *What should you avoid that risks preventing an empowered morning?*

- *What can you do to stop feeling groggy, lazy, and hesitant to get out of bed every morning?*

If you have asked yourself any of these questions, help is finally close at hand!

For a long time, I believed all that mattered was waking up early and heading straight to work. However, I did not have a routine focused on happiness, prosperity, or success; this led to a reactionary approach to life.

My first activity in the morning involved reading and responding to emails—a task I would allocate one hour to, even though it often took much longer. This routine continued for over three years while I was oblivious to how much of a mess it created in my life.

Later, I realized that an unstructured morning often led to a chaotic life and day ahead. This was when I adopted a stable and organized routine—and my life changed for the better.

Over the years, I have experimented with over ten different rituals until I found what works for me. Think of any successful person, be it an athlete, business mogul, actor or actress, musician, politician, or artist. All of them have a morning routine they strictly adhere to, which lays a strong foundation for their day ahead and that they use as a stepping stone to their dreams and aspirations.

You can also be part of this exclusive club. First, let us seek some clarity about a morning routine and morning habits.

Here's Peter

Peter is a middle-aged man who lives in Redmond, Seattle, with his wife, two kids, and an Irish Setter. Peter and his family reside in a townhouse within a suburban community, and he drives 45 minutes to and from work every day. Peter's is your average middle-class American family. Every morning, he wakes up, shaves, brushes his teeth, showers, eats his breakfast, kisses his wife and kids goodbye, gets into his car, and drives to work. That is Peter's morning routine.

Whether you consider it good or bad, a routine consists of a standard set of behaviors conducted repeatedly, and in most cases, they are habitual. Peter's morning routine is familiar to most people who can relate to having a morning routine that involves running out of the door at the last minute, a coffee mug in one hand and a briefcase filled with lots of unfinished paperwork in the other.

If you think about Peter's morning routine, what if it was slightly different? What impact would it have on the rest of his day?

According to a study by Duke University, 45% of human behavior is habitual—made up of habits. Therefore, routines primarily consist of patterns that run our lives. That means your driving route to work every morning is a routine entrenched in tradition. So, if a routine is a habit, what exactly is a habit?

Habits entail creating complex pathways involving our brain's neurons, which bridge seemingly unrelated chores into clusters. It is these seemingly unrelated tasks that form the foundation for our habits. With time, as the set of behaviors in a routine is repeated, the traditions and patterns become more deeply grounded in our minds, resulting in more robust neural pathways.

This explains why routines are so important. They are based on habits, which, on their part, control a huge chunk of our behavior. It also becomes clear that if we can influence our practices, we can change our routines and, subsequently, our behavior—and eventually, the outcome and overall quality of our lives.

Numerous studies have also shown that starting your day correctly has many benefits. For example, it can improve the overall quality of your life, health, and sleep, and even help you remain focused and eventually achieve your goals in the long run. That sums up this book's main objective—to show you how to empower your mornings and set yourself up for daily success.

By the end of this book, you should have all the tools and resources you need to change or improve your morning habits by empowering your mornings and eagerly anticipating the bright and limitless prospects every brand-new day promises!

"When you rise in the morning, give thanks for the light, for your life, for your strength. Give thanks for your food and for the joy of living. If you see no reason to give thanks, the fault lies in yourself."

–Tecumseh

Chapter 1

The (Unexpected) Power of Early Rising

"When you change how you wake up in the morning, you change your entire life."

— Hal Elrod

Early risers tend to be dynamic problem-solvers who seem entirely in control of their personal and professional lives.

Have you ever wondered how these morning people achieve so much in just 24 hours? While night owls may dispute this fact and claim it is still possible to get some extra work done at the end of a typical day—an argument that may carry some merit—most of us are hardwired to be most productive in the early hours of the day.

When we talk about waking early, it is essential to point out that you can wake up as early as possible as long as you get the recommended 7-9 hours of sleep. For example, if you wish to start your days at 5 am, you should try to be asleep by around 9 or 10 pm at the latest. According to studies, even waking up one hour earlier than usual can positively impact your day, productivity, and health—and it does not necessarily have to be in the wee hours of the morning.

Most successful people in their respective fields are early risers. That is because the practice gives you a head start on your day, which offers you sufficient time to complete planned work or errands.

Initially, waking up early can feel like a tall order, especially for night owls. However, focusing on its benefits, ranging from improved mental health and better sleep quality to increased productivity, will have you agreeing that cultivating a morning routine is well worth the time, struggle, and effort.

The Science Behind Early Rising

When darkness sets in, our bodies produce a sleep-inducing hormone called melatonin. The sleep-wake cycle activated in our bodies every day is the regulatory purview of our internal clock called the circadian rhythm, a system activated by the light and dark conditions of the day.

When daylight hits your retinas, it signals your body's central biological clock, the Suprachiasmatic Nucleus (SCN), to suppress melatonin production to activate wakefulness. Naturally and by design, we are more alert and responsive during morning hours and sleepy and sluggish at night.

Benefits of Waking Up Early in the Morning

Here are some of the primary benefits of waking up early:

Better mental state

Research has shown that waking up early can improve cognitive functions because most people are usually more alert and have better and longer concentration levels in the morning. Interestingly, there is also a possible link between early risers and success.

A 2010 study by Christoph Randler, a biologist, found that morning people are more goal-oriented, have strong problem-solving skills, and are more proactive. Another 2008 study among college students revealed that early risers earned a total grade point higher than those who usually stayed up late.

Studies have shown that early risers have more positive thoughts than night owls and are typically more satisfied with life, optimistic, conscientious, and agreeable. Women who wake up early experience a lower risk of suffering from mental illnesses such as anxiety or depression.

Poor sleep quality often causes low cognitive functions, mood swings, memory, and concentration problems.

Superior sleep quality

Sufficient sleep offers your body enough time to self-repair, improves blood pressure and circulation, and boosts essential brain function, the immune system, and mood.

Being an early riser makes it easier to go to bed early and maintain consistent sleep and wake times, leading to a well-regulated circadian rhythm, which results in a deeper sleep.

Here is how it works;

When you wake up early, you will most probably tire early as well. When you get to bed, sleep comes without a struggle, and you become accustomed to the natural circadian rhythm of early rise and bed.

When you have a consistent sleep pattern, you are less likely to experience bouts of exhaustion during your day. Going to bed early also increases your chances of completing the four sleep cycles that enable you to wake up rejuvenated and refreshed in the morning. People who habitually stay up late are at a higher risk of developing sleep disorders like insomnia and are prone to experiencing chronic fatigue during their day.

It enables you to beat the rush hour

Morning traffic can put you on edge, increase stress and anxiety, and mess up your day's planned schedule due to the unpredictable, chaotic, and slow nature of traffic jams. But if you wake up early, you can leave earlier and beat the morning rush hour. This means you will not waste time stuck in traffic as you head to work and will be on time for all other appointments scheduled throughout the day.

Offers time for a healthy breakfast

When you wake up late and find yourself in a rush every morning, you will most likely barely have enough time to eat a healthy breakfast. Chances are, you will grab an unhealthy snack or forgo breakfast altogether.

According to research, people who sleep late and rise late eat an average of 248 more calories daily, including twice as much fast food and soda and half as many vegetables and fruits than early risers.

Waking up early gives you ample time to prepare and eat a healthy breakfast. Because of this healthy start, you are likelier to arrive at healthier snacking decisions later in the day. This significantly reduces your risk of obesity and other lifestyle health conditions.

Reduces stress levels

Early risers have the advantage of leisurely planning their day ahead, which prevents them from rushing through their day blindly and with a cluttered mind.

The ability to plan your day well ahead of time eliminates the stress associated with rushing to complete tasks or keep appointments. In addition, waking up early offers you some time to engage in activities that mitigate stress, which helps you begin your day with a composed and calm mind.

This enables you to be better equipped to solve problems and prioritize tasks, which are some of the main ingredients for a stress-free day.

Creates time for a fitness session or other activities you enjoy

If your daytime schedule tends to be busy, early mornings may be the best time to slot in a morning workout or any other action you prefer. After a long, demanding, tiring workday, gathering enough motivation to hit the gym can be challenging. This makes it easier to skip an evening workout, but you are not likely to miss out on a morning exercise session.

During morning hours, you are more likely to feel energized, and besides beginning your day on a high note, a morning workout also improves your physical and mental health. Additionally, it enhances your cognitive functions, reduces your risk of heart disease, and regulates weight, moods, and blood sugar, among several other benefits.

According to a 2012 National Library of Medicine study, adults who habitually woke up early showed a more positive attitude and general state of mind than their night owl counterparts. This is because they adopted better morning habits and were well-rested, energetic, punctual, stress-free, and healthier. This sense of having things ordered made them happier.

It leads to better organizational skills

The reason your early morning hours happen to be more productive is that you get uninterrupted time all to yourself. Without distractions, you can complete tasks faster and use this quiet time to plan the day and allocate specific times for every task on your to-do list. Mentally scheduling your day in advance sharpens your organizing skills and increases your level of productivity.

As you can see, waking up early has many surprising benefits. Unfortunately, for most people, waking up early can be challenging.

Let's briefly discuss some key things you can do to start your journey to becoming an "early bird."

How to Begin Your Early Riser Journey

The art of becoming an early riser is not an overnight achievement, and you may find the initial stages a tad difficult. However, it is possible to train your mind and body to wake up early and more efficiently. Some people get so good at choosing their wake-up time that all they have to do is visualize their preferred time before they sleep, and that is the exact time they will wake up—without the help of an alarm clock.

The following tips can help as you begin your journey to becoming an accomplished early riser:

Find a motivating reason to wake up early

Find a motivator to wake up early and spend your morning doing something meaningful and of value to you. It could be a workout session, cooking your favorite meal, or even gardening before you officially start your day. Failure to have a good reason to wake up early may cause your addled brain to justify sleeping in.

Make small, gradual changes

Sudden and abrupt changes can be mentally and physically overwhelming and result in crashes. For example, it is not advisable to wake up one day at 4 am when your average time is 11 am. Instead of such an approach, gradually increase the time you wake up earlier. For example you can make small, incremental changes to your original wake-up time, stretched over several days or weeks. This way, you give your body sufficient time to adjust to the new sleep pattern and any other adverse effects that may arise from this change, such as sleep deprivation, fatigue, or sleep inertia, which minimizes the impact.

Come up with a sleep schedule

Develop a consistent sleep schedule to improve the timing of your circadian rhythm, which will result in getting tired early in the evening and waking up around the same time each day. Ensure your new sleep schedule allows you to get an average of 7-9 hours every night.

Adopt good sleep hygiene practices

Sleep hygiene is about healthy practices and habits that facilitate sleep. Examples of some ways you can encourage good sleep hygiene include:

- Avoiding vigorous workout sessions late at night

- Ensuring your bedroom is dark, quiet, and cool

- Limiting the use of blue light electronics, such as phones and laptops, to at least one hour before bedtime

- Not eating heavy and oversized meals just before retiring

- Ensuring you eat whole, healthy meals and lots of water during the day

- Having a relaxing bedtime routine in place

- Sleeping on a quality mattress that is comfortable and equally distributes your weight

Improving your sleep hygiene ensures that getting quality sleep every night is more straightforward, in addition to waking up early in the morning.

Place your alarm clock some distance from the bed

Placing your alarm clock next to your bed makes it easier to hit snooze and continue sleeping—and you wake up two hours later, cursing yourself yet again and having no choice but to rush through your morning.

However, if you place the clock some distance away, where you have to get out of bed to switch it off, your chances of hitting snooze and returning to bed are lower, and your morning routine can begin on time.

Leave your bed immediately

Your brain is hardwired to recognize and link places and activities. For example, your brain becomes aware that you will probably get a bite whenever you walk into the kitchen.

After waking up every morning, it is essential to stretch and get out of bed immediately. If you continue lying awake in bed, your brain may associate your bed with a resting place instead of a place to sleep, making sleeping on your bed difficult.

Also, the more you lie awake in bed, the more difficult getting out becomes, and there is a high possibility that you may slip back into slumber.

Learn to enjoy the early morning

Early mornings have a lot to offer, even though most of us underappreciate this time of day. The quiet serenity provides you time to enjoy your own company and thoughts, which are some rarer privileges mornings extend.

Try stepping out into the morning light and allowing the direct sunlight to activate your circadian rhythm, which will make you feel energized and tired in the evening and enable you to sleep early. Or you can open the windows and let the fresh morning light and air in. These simple activities are similar to taking a happiness pill every morning.

However, you should note that waking up early amounts to little if your morning activities or routines are not productive and beneficial to your day ahead and overall goals.

Remember, I was always an early riser but indulged in all the wrong activities before discovering the secret of a morning routine. Therefore, it is crucial to combine early rising with productive, healthy, and meaningful practices that enable you to enjoy all the benefits of a morning routine.

"Waking up this morning, I smile. 24 brand new hours are before me. I vow to live fully in each moment."

– Thich Nhat Hanh

Chapter 2

Benefits of a Morning Routine

"If you win the morning, you win the day."

Tim Ferris, entrepreneur/best-selling author

You probably want a morning routine that works for you, but you may still need to decide how or where to begin. It is also possible that you don't consider yourself a 'morning person' (just yet), but all the same, you wish to explore the prospect, how it may look or sound to you, and if there is a reasonable likelihood of finding a morning ritual that works.

Right now, you feel your mornings border on chaos and appear crazy and disorganized, and you would love to restore some sanity and order to the beginning of your day.

Whatever your motivation may be, developing a morning routine that is in tandem with your desired lifestyle is essential in maintaining a healthy work and life balance.

Ideally, you want to start your day feeling energized and refreshed enough to take on whatever life throws at you.

Here are the core benefits of building a solid morning ritual:

Calms morning anxiety

Mornings—even just the thought of them—make many people cringe. This hate for mornings is one of the reasons many people struggle to get out of bed in the morning.

Surprisingly, this is a familiar feeling caused by varied factors like relationship issues, stress at work or school, low self-confidence, and many other problems that eventually lead to anxiety.

Morning anxiety can also be due to having too many obligations, poor planning, a lack of proper time management practices, or the absence of set boundaries.

No matter its cause, morning anxiety can be overwhelming and ultimately cause physical, mental, and emotional health conditions. However, mornings do not have to be this painful.

Although anxiety can occur during other times of the day, most people experience it mainly in the morning. There is a scientific reason for this.

Your body's production of cortisol—the stress hormone—is usually at its highest during the early morning hours. Because of this, you are more likely to feel anxious and, as a result, less productive and focused, and this feeling can also last the entire day.

This is where a reliable morning routine can come to your rescue since it can help you get rid of those anxious moments in the morning in the following ways:

- It helps you avoid sources of stressors or potential distractions, such as your computer and phone.

- It can help you in setting and blocking boundaries by shielding your peacetime.

- It improves your mental clarity and promotes a positive mindset

- It encourages self-care by providing ample time to show up for yourself

Simple things such as your alarm clock can also contribute to morning anxiety. If your alarm shocks you awake, adrenalin pumping through your body, your eyes almost popping out, and your heart pumping like you just completed a marathon so early in the morning, consider changing it to a more soothing or subtle sound.

You also need to change your thought process. For example, suppose you have developed negative thought patterns that tend to lean toward the opposing side. In that case, it can easily lead to morning anxiety, especially when your mind awakens and anxious thoughts take over without any conscious attempt to reverse the tide.

First, it is essential to try and identify the thoughts that require an overhaul. Secondly, create unique and positive counter-statements for every negative review that suddenly surfaces in your mind.

For example, if your first thought in the morning goes something like this, "Oh no! I feel terrible. Will I even make it to work today? How will I get through this day?" Replace such a negative and self-defeating thought with something self-assuring along these lines, "I may feel a little anxious today, but it's not the first time, nor will it be the last, and I've handled it before. Anxiety is normal, and I need to relax and maintain focus. I've got this."

Although this technique takes time and requires much practice, eventually, you will change those negative thought patterns and, in their place, plant positive thoughts accompanied by supporting behaviors to match.

Fosters healthy habits

Once you set up a morning routine and see it through, it allows you to go through the motions of healthy habits on autopilot. As you maintain your way, you will be pleased by how you will be including other healthy habits over time that should continue to add value to your day and life.

Bad morning habits often trickle down to your day-to-day life—the same case with positive habits. That is why it is better to go for a walk, jog, run, journal, or read in the morning rather than pick up your phone to go through social media.

Bad habits tend to waste time, which is usually scarce, especially in the morning. But with a good morning ritual, you will find it easier to avoid harmful habits because your activities are on the clock. Also, this is when you can identify areas in your life you may have neglected.

For example, you may find that once a routine is in place, you start eating a healthier and substantial breakfast, have time for a quick workout, or practice mindfulness—activities that were nonexistent before. These newfound habits often positively influence and extend to other aspects of your day and life.

It gives you total control

Most people have tight schedules, and the resultant attempt to create the perfect work-life balance usually falls flat. When you have to juggle many commitments, something important is bound to suffer in the long run. Often, things can get so thick that you may feel like matters at hand are way above your neck and the days are controlling you—instead of the other way around.

Although the time available in the morning tends to be short and only represents a small part of your day, with an effective morning routine, you can reflect on the tasks or responsibilities ahead and take total control.

This allows you to take stock of the expectations at hand, choose what is essential, what can wait, and which activities you can do without to help you prioritize. Because of this, you plan purposefully and work methodically through each task, which helps ensure you don't feel like you are simply going through the motions like a remote-controlled zombie.

Increases your level of productivity

A well-organized and executed morning ritual allows you to begin your day positively. Each minute is spent on a meaningful and valuable activity right from the word go. If this cycle repeats throughout the day, you avoid wasting time. Additionally, you are likelier to begin, offer your undivided attention to, and complete every task you intend to conduct instead of undertaking several chores and leaving a large majority unfinished.

With a focused and calm mindset, you will notice that the quality of your work or activities will improve significantly—surpassing your set targets and expectations is not uncommon.

At the end of your day, you will be happy to discover you managed to achieve most of what you set out to do—and probably much more. This offers you peace of mind and a sense of satisfaction, which makes you look forward to the following day, allowing you to come up with new plans for the coming 24-hour period. It also leaves you feeling relaxed, without the unnecessary pressure pending issues can bring.

Since morning rituals entail waking up earlier than usual, it increases your day hours, buying additional time to accomplish more.

Prepares you for the day ahead

As proven by the research study that involved customer care staff cited earlier, how you begin and spend your morning influences the rest of your day.

If your day starts on a lazy, chaotic, or rushed note, you should expect your day to follow suit.

However, from the moment you wake up and get out of bed, a morning routine will ensure you are on track, prevent you from wasting precious time, and provide you with the right frame of mind—and it stays that way for the remainder of your day.

Boosts your energy levels

Most people detest mornings because of the low energy levels they experience so early in the day. A morning ritual can give you back your lost energy, especially primarily if the activities involved are conducted reliably and spontaneously, allowing no time to feel lazy.

Also, meditation and a short but high-intensity workout capped by a cold shower can leave you feeling invigorated and refreshed, and work wonders on your low energy levels. In a nutshell, including activities you enjoy in your morning ritual will motivate you, stimulate enthusiasm, and automatically activate your energy levels.

Battles poor memory

A morning routine is usually a systematic, step-by-step, pre-planned, and well-thought-out set of activities you conduct every morning. For example, after waking up, your schedule may include a 30-minute walk, taking the trash out, a shower, a little reading, preparing breakfast, dressing, dropping the kids to school, and heading to work—in that exact order.

The chances of forgetting something, say, taking out the trash, decrease considerably if you religiously follow the same daily routine cycle. You do not even have to stop and think if you left out or missed anything because your morning ritual will be so ingrained in your mind that you perform your morning activities like clockwork.

Incidents and scenarios such as arriving at work only to realize you forgot something important become a thing of the past. Also, the small tasks that often pass recollection, such as leaving your tap or lights on, forgetting to lock your home door, or feeding your pet, will rarely be accidentally skipped.

Forgetful situations usually occur when a morning routine is absent or of little personal interest to you. But a morning ritual that fills you with enthusiasm usually is efficient as it invigorates, stimulates your brain, and provides a much-needed surge of energy, which sharpens your cognitive functions.

Enhances confidence

You tend to feel more confident whenever you are relaxed, calm, collected, and in control. Confidence in yourself and your abilities at this early stage of the day improves your emotional and mental health. As a result, it places you in a better position to handle and overcome challenges, setbacks, hurdles, conflicts, and stressful situations that may arise—all of which can potentially ruin an otherwise lovely day.

A morning routine ensures prudent time management practices are put to good use, which can translate to achieving more and boosting your self-esteem even further.

For example, once you create time dedicated to personal self-care, you tend to pay more attention to detail. This means you do not rush through grooming activities like making your hair, applying makeup, choosing what to wear, and dressing, which surrounds you with a positive aura, ensuring you feel good about yourself.

It enables you to be flexible, creative, and accommodating

There is always a possibility that your morning routine might go differently than planned. You may have to change or modify your original plans, include a habit or activity not initially on the menu, or exclude one that appeared in your day's to-do list, mainly since your morning ritual represents the beginning of your day, and sticking to it is essential. But if matters get out of hand, you will find it easier to cope and adapt to the unexpected turn of events.

This improves your ability to be versatile, think on your feet, make quick decisions or choices, and practically exercise your problem-solving skills on short notice. If the rest of your day also turns out the same way, you will be better prepared to implement the same flexible and open-minded approach to weather any storm that threatens to come to your practice effectively.

Also, your ability to learn how to adapt your morning routine around emerging issues is a vital skill that you can apply to several other aspects of your daily life.

Instills discipline

As we have discovered, a morning routine involves careful, thoughtful planning, prioritizing, practicing time management, and military precision execution of your preferred activities that help you achieve your immediate and long-term goals. The art of creating, committing, and going through with your morning routine ensures you strive to make it work by strictly concentrating on activities that matter for the sake of the bigger picture, sacrificing, and doing away with liabilities and things that threaten to derail your plans and goals.

This is an act of good intent to improve your life, which requires much determination, focus, a healthy dose of self-control, and dedication to be effective and finally register success. This is because the envisioned results will not be visible instantly. But through your daily morning routine, any improvements will require you to be consistent and to put in the hard work daily for the fruits of your labor to become evident with time. This instills discipline in your mornings with a good chance of being adopted and becoming a permanent and valuable feature in other facets of life.

Improves quality of life

As we have learned, bad and good habits can take over and dominate your life, depending on your choices and the lifestyle you choose to lead.

However, by and large, most morning routines consist of good habits that can spill over to other areas of your life. Additionally, adopting these good habits acts as a stepping stone in your journey to achieving your life goals—which are also positive.

Therefore, a morning routine can gradually help you overwrite destructive habits such as unhealthy eating, addictions, and sedentary lifestyles. It can help you replace these habits with activities that offer a better lifestyle, improved health, and longevity in the short and long term.

For example, when you introduce regular workouts in your morning ritual, the activity comes with health benefits such as boosting your immunity and preventing lifestyle diseases and conditions like type 2 diabetes and obesity.

It also minimizes the risk of strokes and heart illnesses, among other potentially life-threatening conditions. Due to this, you get sick less often because your immunity is more robust, keeping obesity, heart ailments, and diabetes at bay, owing to a healthier you.

This upbeat, morning-routine-aided change improves the overall quality of your life in all departments. It allows you to age gracefully and considerably increase your years in this world, granting you the rare privilege of seeing your great-grandchildren.

Strengthens relationship bonds

"I can't make you happy unless I am," is a factual and common saying. When you cannot positively focus on your life or are constantly stressed, it is impossible to spread joy and positively impact the lives of loved ones—whether it is family, friends, spouse, close acquaintances, or colleagues. We

typically radiate how we feel, and negative and positive energies are highly contagious.

But if you are happy, content, organized, ambitious, optimistic, booming with health, generally living your life to the fullest, and enjoying every moment in the process—traits that a morning routine cultivates—then you possess the power to influence the lives of others positively and strengthen the respective relationship bonds you share with them. You can also be a role model to many and inspire others to follow your positive, healthy, go-getter, purposeful, helpful, and goal-oriented approach to life.

Why Should You Adopt a Morning Routine?

Here are some core reasons why you should empower your mornings with an effective morning routine:

Unravel your reason for waking up every morning

Why do I need to do this? The answer to this question is essential if you wish to reap the benefits of a morning ritual, especially if you link your long-term goals to the habit(s) you aim to cultivate each morning.

Everybody has a long-term goal(s), often hazy and unclear. As a result, it makes it challenging to articulate practical and tangible steps required to place the purpose(s) within reach. However, carefully calibrating your objectives will help you stay motivated courtesy of your morning routine. Apart from assisting you to make progress towards your goals, a morning ritual also places you firmly in the driver's seat of your destiny and life.

According to two research studies (Azjen 2006; Chou & Chi 2001), participants who displayed a strong sense of control were more likely to experience a significant degree of fulfillment and seemingly led happier lives.

Therefore, set clearly defined goals depending on your plan, whether investing, losing weight, or walking down the aisle shortly. Make sure that it holds much meaning on a personal level to ensure you remain focused in your morning ritual.

This creates a sense of purpose that acts as the wind beneath your wings and powers your morning ritual, leading to an optimal start to your day.

How You Feel in the Morning

How you feel in the morning significantly influences how you will mostly feel during your day.

According to a study by the University of Pennsylvania, customer service employees were likelier to rate their clients during their morning sessions. They were also more positive about themselves during this timeframe. This led to an observation that their mood directly connected to their positive perception personally, extended to their customers, and reflected their feelings for the rest of the day.

On the other hand, managers' positive feelings increased employees' performance, leading to more completed work—and interestingly, of better quality.

A strong proponent of this study would be Hal Elrod, the author of the bestseller, *Miracle Morning*. In his book, he describes the impact of how you start your day as follows:

"How you wake up each day and your morning routine (or lack thereof) dramatically affects your levels of success in every single area of your life. Focused, productive, successful mornings generate focused, productive, successful days—in the same way, unfocused, unproductive, mediocre days, and ultimately a mediocre quality of life. Changing how you wake up in the morning can transform any area of your life faster than you ever thought possible."

While it may sound over-enthusiastic or exaggerated, it is essential to understand the author's background.

Morning rituals transformed Hal Elrod from bankrupt and depressed to a successful businessman, bestseller, highly sought-after keynote speaker, and ultra-marathon runner.

Elrod's teachings on utilizing morning routines to achieve goals faster have inspired millions worldwide to embrace morning rituals.

Give Your Mornings a Personal Touch

It is important to note that a one-size-fits-all approach to morning rituals does not exist. While what worked for Hal Elrod may be a good source of inspiration, it may be ineffective in your case or current circumstances. Therefore, it is vital to set personalized goals and begin by taking baby steps toward their actualization over a given duration.

To achieve this, the trial and error method would be a great place to start. Patiently experiment with various morning routines and watch if they bring you within striking distance of your goals—let go of those that don't and hold on to the ones that do.

Although it is essential to maintain a certain level of consistency, on some mornings, it is common to miss or take an occasional break from your morning rituals. Do not be too harsh on yourself when this happens—you are only human, and it is quite okay. Sometimes, even the best-laid plans fail to materialize. The idea is not to attempt to be perfect but to create a system that leads to gradual improvement.

However, developing such a system and ensuring its effectiveness is not a walk in the park. It requires a practical approach and an active strategy to ensure the benefits have a long shelf-life. It needs more than just willpower. It is also about building an intricate and intelligent brain neurological system.

Also worth noting is that it takes around 66 days on average for a new habit to be fully adopted, such as working out, if performed at least 30 minutes every day (Lally et al., 2010). Consistency and patience are crucial if you wish to permanently stamp that coveted activity into your morning routine.

How Forming a Morning Habit Works

Which activity do you usually engage in every morning immediately after you wake up? Hit the shower, go through your phone, open your social media accounts, read emails or respond to them, exercise, take a walk, or lie in bed wishing every day was a weekend? Whatever you choose to do is crucial and matters more than you may think.

Whether you consider it a morning habit, routine, ritual, or custom, if you consistently and correctly implement the activity(s) you choose to kick-start your day, it can hugely impact your life's direction. This has the backing of research studies, many showing that adopting a conformable morning ritual can improve your overall performance, increase your happiness level, boost self-confidence, help you overcome procrastination, and much more.

Repeated actions over a certain period slowly turn into habits. According to Felix Ravaisson, an influential French Philosopher, *'Habits are familiar, yet mysterious,'* and usually possess a curious life of their own. Of particular interest to Ravaisson were adaptive, mindful, or positive habits—the ones we form through our own volition, such as morning habits—as opposed to those we develop unconsciously.

We can approach habit formation subjectively or scientifically. Another French philosopher, Bergson, 1911, divided habits into two categories:

Active habits – These develop owing to our efforts courtesy of repeated intention.

Sedentary habits – These form through exposure to things we get accustomed to. For example, a mountain climber's body will automatically adapt to a high altitude with much lower oxygen levels.

Morning habits fall under the active category that forms the subject of our interest and the group we will dwell on.

On the other hand, there is the technical angle, where neuroscience research (study of the brain, functions, and systems) has achieved significant progress and highlighted the vital brain pathways predominantly involved in forming habits.

"The most efficient way to live reasonably is every morning to make a plan of one's day and every night to examine the results obtained."

– Alexis Carrel

Chapter 3

The Neuroscience Approach to Morning Rituals

"Give every day the chance to become the most beautiful day of your life."

– Mark Twain

When you begin a new morning routine, like working out, on the first day, you will probably find your attempts strenuous, filled with effort, exertion, and quite conscious. As days go by, and with continuous practice, you become skillful and eventually form a habit that you can conduct automatically and quickly, even with other things on your mind.

So, how do goal-oriented and conscious actions form into habits?

According to Yin & Knowlton, 2006, the answer to this mystery is in a part of the brain called the basal ganglia. These are a group of deep subcortical nuclei structures located at the base of the brain that interestingly developed in our nervous system during evolution.

The primary function of these structures is to coordinate all types of voluntary movements, including complex actions ranging from manipulating our hands, walking, talking, grasping, running, eating, and so on.

Because movements are more effective when habitual or learned, this makes the basal ganglia central to habit formation. We form selective habits through the interaction of two well-defined basal ganglia pathways, according to Yin & Knowlton, 2006. These are:

Associative – This pathway deliberately collects information required to achieve specific goals. For example, if you are shivering from cold, you will want to find a way to keep warm.

Automatic – Here, the pathway takes cues learned from the associative path and includes them in a collection of stored habits. Therefore, whenever you feel cold, you automatically reach for your jacket or another heat source.

The habits will then be available on demand or when prompted by a particular situation. For example, if you jog in the morning, once you start the routine, it triggers the routine of putting on your running shoes in a sequence of actions you are well-acquainted with and, in most cases, automatic.

Another crucial aspect that plays a significant role in habit formation is the reward or positive reinforcement. If you want to turn a specific activity into a habit, apart from performing it repeatedly, it pays to reinforce it positively as well.

It is possible to activate positive reinforcement through an external reward such as patting yourself on the back, remuneration, or a treat such as your favorite food. This causes your brain to release dopamine, a 'feel-good' hormone. Dopamine can be released through internal triggers like envisioning yourself achieving a goal you hold dear, according to Neuroscience News, 2015.

Studies have shown that dopamine release depends on neurons in the limbic system—the brain circuit responsible for emotional processing. Trafton, 2012, posits that the limbic system is interconnected with the basal ganglia and can stamp our memories and habits with reward and emotional value.

The Psychology Behind Morning Habits

William James, an American philosopher, made some of the earliest contributions to habit-forming studies. Some of his early 1900s findings still resonate to this day.

According to James, 1914, *'Habit is the direct consequence of repeating a particular action repeatedly, in similar circumstances to the point it is deeply ingrained in the circuit of the brain.'* Additionally, ingrained habits tend to emerge in the face of solid cues associated with a habit's formation.

Immediately after waking up, you may look at the time and hop out of bed to conduct a particular activity. In this case, the time and movement cue the automatic habit of getting out of bed to complete the training. Later, other behavioral scientists like BF Skinner developed James' work using animal studies. Some of the studies emphasized how rewards fuel habits.

In a 1953 study, Skinner constructed cages for pigeons equipped with buttons that dropped a food pellet when pressed. While exploring the cell, a pigeon would peck the switch at some point in the adventure, only to realize this action produced a food pellet. This observation formed the basis of the primary factors required to create a habit, according to Skinner:

- **Stimulus** – Similar to the pecking of the button

- **Habit** – The action of pecking the button

- **Reward** – The food pellet produced

According to Skinner, 1953, behaviors repeatedly performed for a reward eventually become habits. This theory was attested by the pigeons constantly pecking the button even when this action stopped bringing forth food pellets.

Other hypotheses along the same lines attempted to go beyond only observatory studies and introduced a cognitive or mental aspect in habit formation. Tolman, 1948 & 1954, suggested that habitual or repeated responses utilized internal ideas or 'maps' as cognitive components that assisted in navigating through a maze.

Through technological advances in neuroscience, and with the help of procedures such as brain scans or nerve conduction, further habit-forming questions have been comprehensively addressed. Here are two fascinating studies involving habits and the brain:

Dr. Wendy Wood, a psychologist with the Habit Lab of the University of Southern California, discovered that 43% of the daily activities involved in the study were carried out by participants habitually while thinking of something else (Wood et al., 2002).

For example, you may be in the process of your morning run, but your mind is thinking about how you will take a shower, what you'll have for breakfast, how you will prepare the kids for school, and how you will hit the road. Does that sound familiar?

But how do we know when to begin and stop morning habits when we don't perform some of them consciously?

Neuroscientists at the Massachusetts Institute of Technology (MIT) established that when you perform a morning ritual, such as brushing your teeth, it activates a group of neurons in the basal ganglia, or they 'fire' once you begin the routine. They maintain a low profile and remain silent as you proceed with the training. Once the ritual is complete, the neurons 'fire' again (Martiros et al., 2018).

The study shows that even if your mind is elsewhere when brushing your teeth, it is possible to begin and end a habitual routine automatically because the specialized neurons will guide you through the entire process.

In life, there is always the possibility of making improvements, matters that require solving, places to go, people to see, and issues to solve—regardless of your current stage in life.

Therefore, coming up with and executing a morning routine that matches your lifestyle, goals, and preferences can be a priceless tool that can go a long way in ensuring you tackle your responsibilities, challenges, and objectives efficiently and effectively. This, in turn, translates to a simpler, happier life.

"You can't go back and change the beginning, but you can start where you are and change the ending."

—C.S Lewis

Chapter 4

The Mindset and Early Morning Routines of Highly Successful Performers

"Every morning, I wake up saying, 'I'm still alive, a miracle.' And so I keep on pushing."

— **Jim Carrey**

A large chunk of a morning routine involves your mindset—to get you into the right frame of mind for a positive and productive day ahead. As a result, this enables you to get things done practically and out of the way so you can concentrate on other important matters.

One of the best ways to come up with your morning routine and draw inspiration is to learn and borrow a leaf from the best—well-known personalities worldwide who are highly successful.

Most people begin their day with a very loud alarm clock, a giant steaming mug of coffee, and checking correspondence on their phones or computers.

Interestingly, successful people avoid some of these things as if they were the plague.

Here are some tips that may help you choose the morning habits you would wish to integrate into your early routine.

Ditch the Alarm Clock

What do Amazon CEO, Jeff Bezos, Apple CEO, Tim Cook, and Oprah Winfrey have in common? They do not use alarm clocks and prefer to wake up naturally. Just the word alarm, which means 'a sudden fear or distressing suspense caused by an awareness of danger,' is enough motivation for the trio to steer clear of the gadget.

According to the National Sleep Foundation, the dependency on an alarm clock to wake up every morning signals that you probably did not get the 7-9 hours of recommended sleep.

The startling effect of an alarm clock is that it unnecessarily pumps up your adrenaline and activates a host of stress hormones—which is not the best way to begin your day.

However, that does not imply you should throw away your alarm clock—at least not just yet. The best approach is gradually weaning yourself out of your over-reliance on the gadget by ensuring you get the recommended 7-9 hours of sleep and creating a predictable sleep pattern that your body can naturally adopt over a certain period. With time, you will find that you automatically wake up at the required time every morning, courtesy of your internal body clock, sometimes even before your alarm clock goes off. When this pattern becomes the norm, you can safely ditch your alarm clock without oversleeping.

Apple CEO, Tim Cook, wakes up at 3.45 am every morning without using an alarm clock. Talk show queen, Oprah Winfrey, automatically gets up between 6.02 and 6.20 am each morning using her internal clock.

Drink Water First, Then Coffee

It may seem logical to grab that hot, steaming mug of coffee first thing in the morning. However, experts suggest a glass of water would be the better option. After your body has endured 7-9 hours without water, downing a glass of water immediately after waking speeds up your metabolism and digestion while also hydrating you.

Water is so essential to your body that tissues and organs in your body require the liquid for most of their functions. Because your body constantly loses moisture, it is vital to compensate for this loss to avoid dehydration.

Renowned author and award-winning actress, Cameron Diaz, is a stickler to this rule. She notes that after brushing her teeth, she drinks one liter of water, which she says energizes her in preparation for a hectic day ahead. A glass of water can refresh, revitalize, and enable you to feel more positive throughout your day—then, you can go for your regular cup of coffee.

Reduce Decision-Making Tasks

A hawk-eyed journalist once asked Former President, Barrack Obama, why he wears identical colored suits every morning. He explained that he had chosen to pare down on the decisions he had to make—to concentrate on the most important—and picking which suit to wear each morning was not on his list of priorities. Therefore, he opted to wear only grey and blue suits to reduce non-vital decisions.

Other personalities eliminate decision-making activities in the morning by planning their next day the evening prior. For example, Kenneth Chenault, former American Express CEO, uses his evening to jot down three things he plans to accomplish the next day.

On the other hand, Barbara Corcoran, *Shark Tank* host, uses a similar approach. She divides and rates the three items she intends to achieve the following day as A, B, and C. The 'A' category is where the gold is and includes activities that can propel her business to the next level and increase revenue.

Creating your to-do list for the following day happens to be more time efficient, does away with morning stress, and marks a definitive conclusion to your day, resulting in a more excellent work-life balance.

Move Your Body

Morning workouts are a common feature in the routines of many successful personalities, from Bill Gates, Barrack Obama, and Richard Branson to Gwyneth Paltrow.

For example, Bill Gates prefers to hit the treadmill every morning and multitasks by watching DVDs simultaneously. On the other hand, Paltrow chooses to check and reply to her emails first and then exercise.

Luxury brand Equinox CEO, Niki Leondakis, performs yoga every morning and states, *"I've always known that you have to be physically healthy and strong to be mentally healthy and strong. It's all connected."*

Practice Self-Awareness

An activity that can pave the way for success your entire day is self-reflection. Often, we find ourselves going through our respective lives on auto-pilot, only to realize somewhere down the road that we lost sight of our passions, goals, and core values. A person who knew this too well was the late Steve Jobs.

To avoid such a scenario, he would stand in front of the mirror every morning and ask himself this question; *"If today were the last day of my life, would I want to do what I am about to do today? If the answer is no for too many days, I know I need to change something."*

This self-awareness technique is what makes a genius. Imagine getting up every morning and not feeling enthusiastic about heading to work or facing the day ahead and continuing to feel this way for months or even years. This strongly indicates that something is not right and needs to change.

Wake up at the Same Time Every Morning

Once you get into a consistent morning routine, your circadian rhythm adapts to your sleep pattern and may cause you to wake up simultaneously each morning, including on weekends. If you use an alarm clock, avoid hitting the snooze button repeatedly and going back to sleep for short durations.

This practice tends to confuse your body. It throws off your internal clock, resulting in feeling foggy, low, and sluggish later during the day. Always set your alarm when you need to wake up and strictly adhere to it.

This is a technique Sheryl Sandberg, former Facebook Chief of Operations (COO), swears by and says it enabled her to get to her office at 7 am every day without fail.

Sandberg used a spiral notebook to create her to-do list and usually checked off her list immediately after she got to the office. She once noted that maintaining a consistent schedule enabled her to sleep better and ensured she went to bed at the same time each night—that is by 10 pm, including on weekends.

It is also advisable to stick to your sleep-wake cycle, even on weekends. While the extra hours of sleep may seem bliss, resist the temptation and keep a regular sleep schedule to avoid disrupting your sleep-wake cycle to enjoy more energy and better sleep quality overall.

Strive to Accomplish One Important Task

According to experts, your willpower is at its strongest in the morning. That is why it is essential to attempt or put some effort into at least one activity that can give you a head start on your day. The task you decide to take on should largely depend on and directly connect to your career and personal goals. For example, Ariana Huffington, Jeff Bezos, and Tim Cook prefer to check and reply to their emails.

Alternatively, you can choose an activity like jotting down notes for a meeting scheduled later in the day, an ongoing project, or a personal project. Experts recommend it is better to pick a task that may require some concentration and self-control to complete efficiently because it is bound to enable you to have a more productive day.

Later in the day, your willpower and motivation will most probably dip. At that point, completing that critical task in the morning when you are fresh and invigorated means you won't have to do it later when your focus is weaker, and you are tired and less willing or able to take on a task of such a critical nature.

Practice Meditation

Numerous studies have shown that people who take time to meditate every morning tend to be happier, more successful, and healthier. This is because they begin their day with a calm and focused mindset that sets the tone for the entire day—think Selena

Gomez, Paul McCartney, Ariana, Beyoncé, and Oprah, among several others.

When you begin your day centered, it places you in a better position to tackle challenges and deal with opportunities the day ahead may bring your way. In an interview, Oprah confessed that meditation was one of the *"most life-enhancing things I ever did."*

In 2011, Oprah admitted to bringing a teacher to Harpo Studios to teach the rest of the staff how to meditate. Employees were given two breaks in the day to meditate. She told Dr. Oz, *"(It) brings a kind of energy and an intensity of energy, an intention we have never had before."*

Early morning meditation also promises quick results. According to studies, in just one week of adopting the practice, you should start noticing some of the powerful benefits of meditation. This may include, but is not limited to:

- Lower stress levels

- Reduced depression and anxiety

- Increased energy

- Better sleep quality

- A boost in self-confidence and enhanced self-awareness

- Improved moods

- Less worrying, owing to the calmness of the mind

More good news is that meditation is not time-consuming—you only need as little as 5 to 10 minutes to get started.

Practice Breathing Exercises

Although these are similar to meditation in some ways, breathing exercises are a favorite of several successful personalities and feature in their everyday morning routines. A good example is actress, Tracee Ellis Ross, who has, on several occasions, even gone a step further and shared some of her breathing techniques with her followers on Instagram.

Ross says breathing exercises help *"to connect me to the present moment and to create space in my body."*

PRESS co-founder, Ed Foy, practices the Wim Hof Method—a combination of breathing and cold therapy whose main objective is to help you connect more deeply to your body. This series of breathing exercises involve prolonged breath holds, powerful inhalation, and relaxed exhalation. Some benefits of the Wim Hof method include heightened focus, boosted immunity, reduced stress, and improved sleep quality.

Integrate the 'Reading Power Hour'

Nobody can claim to have inexhaustible motivation reserves, not even the most successful people amongst us. If neglected, motivation levels can dwindle, which is why regular replenishment is essential.

The 'power hour' involves setting aside a certain amount of time every morning (not necessarily an hour as the name suggests) to watch, listen, or read empowering quotes, inspirational anecdotes, or stories.

For example, Ashley Graham, a model and TV presenter, reads excerpts from her favorite inspirational book, *'The Magnificent Word of the Lord,'* which she finds uplifting and allows her to set her intentions for the day.

Even if a religious book is not your cup of tea, research shows that reading something inspirational for at least half an hour every morning can lower your blood pressure and reduce stress.

"Some people dream of success, while other people get up every morning and make it happen."

– Wayne Huizenga

Chapter 5

Building Your Evening Ritual

"Happiness is... not having to set the alarm for the next day!"

Unknown

Early Bed Activities for Early Morning Preparation

An evening routine acts as a precursor and solid foundation for your morning and, ultimately, your day ahead, which makes it equally important.

If you have healthy evening habits, they will have a positive impact on your morning routine. But if you indulge in unhealthy practices in the evening, your morning will be negatively affected.

For example, if you binge-watch your favorite series late into the night while munching on sugary snacks, can you guess how you will feel the following day? On the other hand, what if you spend your evening journaling, a little meditation, and catching up on the rest of your family's day? Can you guess how it would impact your morning?

Therefore, it is evident that your evening and morning routines are directly linked and highly interdependent. This also means that each one of the routines is just as important as the other.

Importance of an Evening Routine

An evening routine should mainly involve relaxation after a grueling day and habits that help you get sufficient sleep for your body to recover adequately.

As we have stressed countless times in this book, getting 7-9 hours of sleep cannot be emphasized enough, and this is one evening routine that requires special attention.

What happens when you fail to get the recommended amount of sleep, and where does an evening routine fit into all this?

Let's discuss this here...

Sleep and Evening Routines

Sleep allows your body to rest and repair and directly impacts your lifestyle and health. You must have experienced a stormy night's rest and woken up the following day feeling like a truck has run you over—exhausted, groggy, slow, and probably moody. Imagine if you woke up every morning feeling this way and still tried to function normally—it is impossible.

Not getting enough sleep can adversely affect all aspects of your life and health. Just one night of sleep deprivation is bad enough and can adversely affect your decision-making abilities and considerably slow down your response time.

It can also significantly hamper your creativity, thought process, and learning skills. Therefore, it is no surprise that after not getting sufficient sleep, we tend to struggle through the next day.

Additionally, studies show that a lack of enough sleep can compromise your immune system, making you susceptible to various ailments, which may also cost you your overall well-being.

There are two main stages of the sleep cycle

- **REM** – This is the stage of sleep where you experience dreams

- **Non-REM** – Involves deep sleep

The non-REM sleep stage is where your brain resets and begins the recovery process in preparation for the next day's learning and thinking. Due to our hectic lives, you may find it difficult to hop into bed and fall asleep immediately after, let alone get 7-9 hours of sleep.

It is a common occurrence for many people to lie there in bed, mind racing for hours on end before finally falling asleep. Now, this is where an evening routine comes in handy to enable you to relax before bedtime, fall asleep early and faster, and achieve all the sleep stages.

Winding Down the Day

An evening routine should give you the time and space to decompress mentally and physically after a long day.

Sometimes, taking your cares, concerns, racing thoughts, worries, and problems to bed with you is inevitable—but this should be the exception, not the norm.

To avoid such a scenario from playing out often, you should develop an evening routine that helps you tie the loose ends of your day and relax. When you get into your bed feeling settled, calm, and relaxed, you have a much better chance of a good night's sleep and waking up feeling well-rested, refreshed, and rejuvenated the following day.

An Evening Routine Sets the Stage for Success

An evening routine that consists of healthy practices is one of the surest ways of setting yourself up for success the next day. It is crucial to understand that what you do or don't do in the evening may either come back to haunt you the following day or act as a stepping stone towards more significant achievements.

At this point, it is essential to note that your evening routine must be manageable and brief. The right approach is to begin consistently developing small healthy evening habits that can help you get a grip on your schedule, enabling you to accomplish more every other week.

Developing an Evening Routine

Suppose you have been taking each night as it comes. In that case, you now need to adopt a series of behavioral patterns and a series of tasks that eventually transform into a routine you conduct every night before retiring for the day.

Change is always challenging, and you may need to practice a lot of discipline, commitment, and passion, set realistic goals, and monitor your progress regularly. Additionally, what is good for the goose is not necessarily good for the gander, especially regarding evening routines. The most crucial objective is identifying what works or doesn't work for you. This will enable you to customize your evening routine based on what works best for you and your circumstances.

Here are some suggestions on tried and tested ways to create an evening routine that will support your early mornings and entire day:

Unwind and relax

After a hard day's work, an ideal evening routine should begin by unwinding and relaxing your body and mind. Identify a few practices or hobbies that can help you relax.

Avoid carrying unfinished work home in the hope of completing it or other activities related to your professional life. Doing this extends your day into the evening instead of bringing it to a conclusion. Restrict your choice of evening practices to those that are personal and positive.

A practice that can help you relax is jotting down a list of events that unfolded during the day that made you feel grateful or happy. According to Ariana Huffington's book, *Thrive*, research shows that doing this can lower stress levels and provide a sense of calm to your night.

Other relaxing activities you can engage in include:

Reading – Lots of people read in the evening. However, The National Sleep Foundation cautions that this should not occur in bed as it can lead to insomnia. But interestingly, some people can read in bed and fall asleep without problems. You can pleasure-read books or magazines featuring shorter articles and avoid reading work-related material. When you read a sentence repeatedly because the message is not sinking or your eyes feel heavy—it is probably a strong indication that it is time to retire.

Meditation or prayer – Prayer and meditation can calm your mind and be specific to your religious beliefs. You can also use guided imagery, an effective relaxation technique that visualizes peaceful, serene, or joyous settings such as a picturesque beach or scenic meadow to invoke a feeling of calmness.

Listening to music – Music is therapeutic, food for the soul, and very relaxing. Of course, your choice of music should match your preferred genre and taste. However, classical music is naturally soothing to a majority of music lovers. Alternatively, you can play relaxing sounds of nature, available on CD and various applications.

Watching a movie or some TV – It feels nice to rest on an easy chair or lie on the couch watching TV. However, try to avoid programs that are too long or too exciting. If you prefer a movie, one you are familiar with may not be as fascinating, but it can make it easier to break away at bedtime. Ensure your screen is not too close to your eyes to prevent light exposure, which can cause problems when it is eventually time to hit the sack.

Stretching – You can also consider yoga or low-impact stretching exercises that are not too strenuous. If the light stretching you engage in makes you break a sweat, then it is not appropriate to feature in your evening routine. Stretching should involve gentle movements that promote complete relaxation in readiness for sleep.

Integrating Self-Care Practices

Incorporating self-care habits into your evening routine can significantly improve your emotional and mental well-being.

Self-care is a broad concept that can take a diverse approach among a cross-section of people. But basically, it is a form of self-love that can range from giving yourself a facial to pampering yourself with a warm, luxurious bath to having a hot or cold nourishing beverage of your choice.

Contrary to popular belief, self-care does not translate to being selfish. Instead, it is an act of self-compassion. Self-care practices have numerous scientifically proven benefits, including:

- Better management of stress

- Increase in happiness

- A longer lifespan

Besides improving your general well-being, evening self-care habits can also improve your relationship with loved ones. This is because the practice encourages you to better yourself, allowing you to extend the resultant 'feel-good feelings' to those around you.

Here are some suggestions on how you can successfully integrate self-care habits into your evening routine:

Prioritize sleep

Sleep is one of the most important aspects of self-care, and this is because it affects your motivation, livelihood, and mood, so self-care practices should have some winding down habits that promote good sleep.

You can begin by setting a specific hour for bedtime and ensuring you adhere to it and avoid any activities like going through your social media handles or checking emails, which has a high probability of making you stay up late unnecessarily.

Allocate specific time for self-care

An effective bedtime routine should allow you to relax and get deep, restorative sleep. As a reminder, you can set alarms or alerts to notify you when it is time to begin your self-care routine.

The ideal duration of a self-care routine can be anywhere from 30 minutes to an hour—but if you can allocate more time, the better.

Ensure consistency

Consistency ensures you reap the maximum benefits of self-care and a healthy evening routine. To achieve success, begin your self-care routine at an exact time every night—this rule also applies to your bedtime.

Maintaining a set routine makes it easier for your brain to shut down when it is eventually time to hit the sack. Regularly repeated practices place your body and mind on 'autopilot,' making it simpler to unwind and relax.

Unplug to unwind

By now, you have probably heard about the adverse effects of blue light, which your favorite gadgets emit. Unfortunately, all you have heard or read is probably factual.

Studies have shown that blue light reduces the production of melatonin—the hormone responsible for making you feel sleepy. If possible, the best move you can make is to get rid of these blue light-emitting gadgets from your bedroom area, including phones, laptops, tablets, and TVs.

Another approach is to conduct a digital detox, which involves staying away from your gadgets earlier in the evening to allow your brain time to unwind from the devices.

Alternatively, you can purchase a pair of blue light-blocking glasses if you require electronic devices to relax. You can also switch your electronic gadgets into night-shift mode and airplane mode.

If you still cannot resist the urge to browse the internet too close to bedtime, in bed, or late at night, you can take more stringent measures—like disconnecting your Wi-Fi.

Make your bedroom a sanctuary for calm

Your bedroom should be inviting, calm, quiet, and comfortable. It should have an ambiance that promotes a relaxed atmosphere.

To enable such an environment, you can use soft, dim lighting, maintain a temperature of between 62 to 75 degrees (F), ideal for sleep, and use comfortable and cozy beddings. If you live in an area where it gets hot at night, consider using bamboo or cotton bedding to stay cooler.

Have a warm beverage

Although experts recommend avoiding drinking coffee, which contains caffeine, or alcohol, there are several beverages you can enjoy and still manage to sleep. Instead of that nightcap, you can consider having a warm glass of milk or decaffeinated tea such as lemon balm, chamomile, valerian root, or lavender.

Take a luxurious shower or bath

Several studies have shown that a warm bath or shower can make you sleepy and is a perfect way to recharge after a long day.

You can promote relaxation by dimming the lights, lighting scented candles, and using luxurious bath products that release relaxing scents. In the background, you can listen to soothing music, your favorite audiobook, or some guided meditation.

Imagine the water washing away all your stress of the day—a visualization technique that can uplift your mood and tune your mind to the right channel required to get sufficient sleep.

Create time to pamper yourself

After your warm bath or shower, take some time to treat yourself to more self-love, which can take many forms—from a foot and hand massage to practicing a skincare routine. Utilize this time to get in sync with your body. Try a facial massage or a face mask to pamper yourself even more.

Grab a good book

Reading a good book that does not require much effort to decipher can serve two purposes—first, reading causes your eyes to tire, enabling you to sleep quickly. Secondly, it keeps you away from your electronic devices. Try to pick a positive and inspiring book that gets you into the right headspace and brings you joy before you retire.

Try your hand at journaling

Journaling is about putting your thoughts on paper and is a great way to get rid of and prevent bedtime anxiety. It also allows you to let go of any stress you may be experiencing. Always having a notepad and pen on your bedside table can go a long way in encouraging the practice of self-expression before getting into bed.

Embrace mindfulness or meditation

Including meditation in your evening routine is scientifically proven to eradicate insomnia. According to research, it enables you to release stress or built-up tension and encourages you to focus on the present moment. You can use videos, podcasts, or mindfulness apps to promote relaxation if you need to become more familiar with how to do it.

Alternatively, you can focus on breathing and imagine your stress dissolving with every breath. Adding purpose to your mindfulness actions can help you feel grounded and prevent you from feeling overwhelmed. Meditating before slipping into bed can prepare you for a joyous new day.

Plan Ahead

Prepare for the next day by creating a to-do list detailing the activities you intend to carry out in your day. Planning enables you to gain clarity and ensures your morning routine flows smoothly.

When you know the activities you wish to perform, you are bound to save much time. Going to bed with some uncertainty about the following day can cause unnecessary worry and endless tossing and turning in bed, affecting the quality of your sleep.

"I get up every morning, and it's going to be a great day. You never know when it will be over, so I refuse to have a bad day."

– Paul Henderson

Chapter 6

How to Create Amazing Mornings

"If you do not pour water on your plant, what will happen? It will slowly wither and die. Our habits will also slowly wither and die if we do not allow them to manifest. You need not fight to stop a habit. Just don't allow it to repeat itself."

— Sri S. Satchidananda

Experts have found that living a healthy and better life requires avoiding a few things that can potentially harm your morning routine or gravitate into bad habits. At face value, some may seem harmless, but they can easily ruin your day, lower your productivity, or waste precious time without adding value to your morning routine.

A good example is the habit of hitting the snooze button several times, with research showing that it causes you to begin a new sleep cycle that your body is not accustomed to. As a result, you end up feeling exhausted. However, morning routines should make you feel positive, energized, and motivated and increase productivity.

If you want to enjoy these benefits, it is essential to ditch habits that may be detrimental to this objective and replace them with healthy habits.

Hitting the Snooze Button

This ranks as the number one habit you should avoid, owing to how widespread it is.

According to a past survey, one in three adults is guilty of hitting the snooze button every morning at least three times on average, while more than half of adults in their 20s to early 30s admitted to pressing the snooze button every morning.

While it is not such a big deal to get a few extra minutes of sleep on some mornings, regularly engaging in a tug-of-war with your alarm clock comes with the risk of leaving you feeling more tired during the day and may lead to sleepless nights.

Here is how it happens:

Before we can deeply understand how the snooze button ends up being detrimental, we must comprehend how the sleep cycle works and how this action negatively affects it.

Immediately after you hit the pillow at night, you are drowsy, and after a few minutes, you fall asleep. This is the light sleep stage, where your temperature drops and your heart rate slows. The deep sleep stage soon follows, which is a crucial phase because this is where your body strengthens your immune system, regrows tissue, and builds muscles and bones.

From deep sleep, you transition to REM sleep— an abbreviation for Rapid Eye Movement. Here, your brain is super active, so active that you may experience intense dreams.

However, despite the intense brain activity, REM sleep is highly restorative and helps you remain focused and sharp the next day. Getting the right amount of slumber at this stage is imperative. Usually, you experience your REM sleep in the first cycle, 90 minutes after you switch off, and the processes alternate throughout the night.

Where does hitting the snooze button fit into all this?

When your alarm sounds in the morning, you are in the last stages of your final REM sleep cycle. When you wake up, the REM cycle ends. However, pressing the snooze button takes you back to your REM cycle, and when the alarm goes off again, it interrupts you in the middle of your REM sleep instead of towards the end. This is why you may wake up confused, disoriented, and foggy—which is not a healthy way to begin your day.

There is more...

If you went to bed early the previous night, your body's internal clock usually prepares you to wake up when your alarm goes off. Hitting the snooze button throws your entire body into a baffling tailspin. If this continues for a long time, you lose track of your sleep pattern, and it becomes difficult for your body to figure out your sleep-wake times. Thus, when you get into bed at night, you begin tossing and turning, compromising your sleep quality. One week of repeatedly hitting the snooze button is enough to set off this series of events.

To stop this habit, you need to get to the bottom of why you hit the snooze button in the first place. It could be for several reasons. For example, it could be that you're not getting enough sleep. Living a sedentary life, getting too excited before sleeping (thanks to activities like social media), and your bedroom being uncomfortable can all contribute. In a worst-case scenario, you may have a chronic sleep condition.

The only lasting solution, and unpopular for obvious reasons, to avoid repeatedly pressing the snooze button is to hop out of bed immediately after your alarm clock goes off. While it may initially feel unpleasant, the foggy and groggy feeling usually lifts within minutes—leaving you fresh and invigorated to face a new day.

Try adopting the mantra: *You snooze, you lose.*

Heading Straight into Social Media

Although technology came to make our lives easier and more productive and to improve the overall quality of our lives, it can also be a source of stress and a significant distraction if not utilized in moderation.

Your smartphone should be a good servant—not a master of your life. The lack of control over smartphones can negatively affect productivity and social and mental health. Statistics paint a gloomy and alarming picture.

According to an IDC study, a whopping 80% of smartphone owners check their gadgets within 15 minutes, on average, of waking up—which is a huge problem.

When you check your phone immediately after waking up, it bombards you with large volumes of information that require processing, creating stimuli that lead to anxious and stressful thoughts.

On waking up, external stimuli instantly fight for your attention, which does not give you the time or space to begin your day in a calm, focused, and relaxed mode. You lose control of your day when you grab your phone immediately after waking up.

A study by the University of Gothenburg measured the effects of mobile phone use over a year and found high usage directly related to increased depression in both men and women.

Therefore, avoid having a morning and day that feels anxious, rushed, or stressed by not checking your phone for at least one hour after waking up. This is because checking messages, emails, and social media immediately after waking up allows other people's requests and opinions (including advertisements) to pollute your mind. As a result, the information you receive hijacks your thinking. This forces you to begin your day reacting to other people's issues instead of proactively—concentrating on your personal goals.

In Julie Morgenstern's book, 'Never Check Email in The Morning,' the author posits, "...you'll never recover. Those requests, interruptions, surprises, reminders, and problems are endless.... Very little cannot wait a minimum of 59 minutes."

But what exactly happens? Why does checking your social media, messages, and emails affect you this way? There is a compelling scientific explanation:

When you open your social media pages, messages, or emails, your body releases a neurochemical called dopamine that makes you feel rewarded. Interestingly, the brain has a natural craving for dopamine, and any action that releases the chemical will stimulate repetitive behavior so the brain can get that dopamine hit.

Therefore, in a nutshell, the minute you begin aimlessly scrolling through social media or any other platforms, your brain will stimulate you to replicate this behavior repeatedly throughout your day. Fighting against brain cravings will probably end up a losing battle—with all the odds stacked against you.

One way to avoid this habit is to put your phone in flight mode before bed. When you switch it on in the morning, messages, emails, and notifications will begin streaming slowly; they usually take time.

Another effective way is to have at least seven replacement activities, such as exercising, writing, making coffee, and mindfulness, to mention a few. Pick one activity for each day of the week to keep things exciting and avoid monotony. If you do not have a fascinating exercise, you will probably fall back on your smartphone to check social media—and ultimately ruin your day.

Stretch Your Body

Stretching every morning immediately after waking up has numerous benefits, such as helping your body wake up, boosting flexibility, increasing alertness, and easing stress. This is because the act of stretching loosens your muscles and, in the process, improves mobility.

Although there has been very little research on the benefits of stretching, anecdotal evidence alludes to gains like improving moods and easing pain, which is especially helpful for those who sit behind a desk all day with limited movements.

Stretching is so versatile that you can do it anywhere, including in bed, and all you need is five to ten minutes, and you are good to go. That is a small price if you consider the consequences of not getting a good stretch every morning.

Most people associate stretching with gymnasts and athletes, but the truth is that we all need to stretch each morning to preserve our independence and mobility. Physical therapists suggest that stretching should not only be done occasionally—it should be a daily morning activity.

Stretching enables your muscles to remain flexible, strong, and healthy and helps maintain your joints' range of motion. Without it, your muscles become rigid and shorten as a result. When this happens, when you require the use of your muscles, you will find they are weak and unable to extend, placing you at risk of muscle damage, joint strains, and pain. For example, if you sit at a desk all day, your hamstrings tend to tighten, making it difficult to stretch or extend your knee fully, potentially making walking difficult.

Additionally, when you suddenly expose muscles in this condition to strenuous activity, like running or playing tennis, which stretches them, they may damage, owing to the amount of stretching involved. Injured muscles usually do not have the strength to support joints, which can also lead to joint injuries.

On the other hand, a regular morning stretch routine ensures your muscles remain lean, strong, and flexible. Any exertion you may experience during your day will not apply too much pressure on your joints to cause damage if you stretch regularly.

Having strong and healthy muscles also plays a vital role in balancing and avoiding falls.

How to begin your stretching routine

According to experts, while stretching may seem daunting because of the many involved muscles, it is not necessary to stretch every muscle in your body when starting.

Begin with the critical areas that aid mobility—the lower extremities, including the front of your thighs (quadriceps), calves, hip flexors (in the pelvis area), and hamstrings. Later, you can graduate to your upper extremities—your lower back, shoulders, arms, and neck.

Aim to have a daily morning stretching routine or stretch three to four times per week. If you have a condition such as arthritis or Parkinson's disease, it is essential to have your doctor okay your stretching routine before making it a part of your morning routine.

It is also essential to know that stretching on one or two days will not offer you the flexibility and muscle health required. You must be consistent over a certain period and remain committed to the process, which may take weeks to a few months.

Try holding each stretch you execute for at least 30 seconds, and avoid bouncing, which may cause injuries. Every time you stretch a muscle, you are bound to feel the tension—never pain, which could signal tissue damage or injury.

Skipping Breakfast

Fact: Breakfast is the most important meal of the day.

Nutritional guidelines state that missing breakfast daily increases your risk of obesity. Despite this, up to a quarter of Americans skip breakfast, according to Kant and Graubard, 2015.

Studies also reveal that people who have their breakfast every morning tend to be healthier and with a lower risk of being overweight or obese and also avoid contracting several chronic diseases. Moreover, individuals who eat breakfast also gravitate towards more nutritious diets and consume more micronutrients and fiber.

Some research studies also suggest that serial breakfast skippers usually have unhealthy habits, such as sedentary lives, excessive alcohol consumption, and smoking, Cahill et al., 2014.

To serve as an inspiration and ensure you integrate a healthy breakfast into your morning routine, here are a few consequences of skipping the day's most important meal:

Causes your blood sugar levels to drop

In a literal sense, breakfast 'breaks the fast' after a rest-filled night. A healthy breakfast restores your glycogen and stabilizes your insulin levels. Failing to have breakfast also fails to replenish your glucose levels, often leading to extreme hunger, fatigue, and irritability.

Slows your metabolism

Studies show that eating breakfast encourages your body to burn more calories during the day. However, when you do not eat breakfast, your body does the opposite—it hoards large amounts of calories in preparation for a period of potential starvation. Your metabolism slows, and your body turns to glucose stored in your muscles to act as fuel, which results in your muscles wasting away.

Increased stress hormones production

A healthy breakfast has a positive impact on the production of cortisol—which is the primary stress hormone.

Cortisol levels are usually at their highest around 7 am, and eating breakfast inhibits the production of cortisol to low levels. When cortisol levels are high, you tend to feel anxious or nervous for no apparent reason.

Increases your risk of heart ailments

Regularly skipping breakfast exposes you to weight gain and the risk of high cholesterol, obesity, heart disease, diabetes, atherosclerosis (build-up of harmful fats on your artery walls), and high blood pressure.

A 16-year research study found that people who opted to skip breakfast were 27% more likely to suffer from heart attacks or coronary heart disease—the most common cause of death.

The most common reason why many people skip breakfast is not feeling hungry. If this sounds familiar, begin your day with a healthy smoothie or milkshake. Also, avoid heavy dinners by keeping your portions small, not snacking before bedtime, and reducing alcohol in the evening to enable a healthy morning routine.

Brushing Your Teeth After Eating

Dental care experts opine that the best time to brush your teeth is before breakfast. If you must brush them after breakfast, wait at least 30 minutes because foods contain acids, and if you brush immediately after breakfast, you weaken the enamel of your teeth, which is the outer layer.

Also, there is a misconception that toothbrushes with stiff bristles clean your teeth better. The opposite is actually true—soft bristles are more effective cleaners. Stiff bristles can also wear out your enamel and may cause your gums to recede due to their abrasive nature.

Leaving Your Bed Unmade

Although it's a straightforward chore, making the bed in the morning is one of the most neglected tasks by people. However, taking a few minutes each morning after getting up to make your bed has numerous rewards worth your time. Here's why:

Maintains cleanliness

Making your bed removes dust, and covering your bed with a duvet or bed cover reduces the surface area where dust can accumulate. If you have a pet, making your bed ensures it only has access to your bed's topmost layer, keeping any messes or fur shedding to a minimum.

Assists in the adoption of healthier habits

Making your bed can serve as a 'keystone habit' that can lead to a domino effect in picking healthier practices by making other intelligent choices during your day.

According to the bestseller, *The Power of Habit,* by author Charles Duhigg, *"Making your bed every morning correlates with better productivity, a greater sense of well-being, and stronger skills to sticking to a budget. It is not that a family meal or a tidy bed causes better grades or less frivolous spending. But somehow those initial shifts start chain reactions that help other good habits take hold."*

Starts your day on a positive note

It feels great to complete one task immediately after waking up. This small achievement can help you face the day ahead with a sense of accomplishment, even before you embark on the rest of your morning routine.

Enables better sleep

A routine poll by the National Sleep Foundation found that people who reported making their bed every morning were more likely to experience better sleep quality. This supports another NSF finding establishing that maintaining a clean-looking bedroom can hugely impact the quality of your slumber.

"When each day is the same as the next, it's because people fail to recognize the good things that happen in their lives every time the sun rises."

– The Alchemist

Chapter 7

Building Your High-Performance Morning Routine

"A high-performance morning routine sets you up for a productive day, which leads to more wins. More wins increase your motivation, allowing you to accomplish your goals more easily."

— Danny Forest

As we have already established, your morning routine should be unique to your specific needs and goals. Your wake and sleep times do not have to match others'. We cannot all wake up at the same time; neither can we all have the same goals.

However, a few key things remain constant across all morning routines. For example, a morning routine should consist of predominantly healthy and positive activities that add value to your life, help you achieve your goals, and enable you to be a better version of yourself. Consequently, you should consistently perform these pre-determined morning activities to form positive and healthy habits.

Therefore, a robust and high-performance morning routine should work for you and pave the way for your day to accomplish meaningful and immediate results. Your training should also help you to remain motivated throughout the day.

Another point worth noting is that the time you have in the morning is limited and should consist of critical and high-priority activities that enable you to achieve high productivity levels. That is where the 20-80 approach can come in handy.

It entails identifying and performing 20% of the activities that will provide you with 80% of the results you desire. Moreover, it helps you to be aware of the order in which you perform your activities for maximum effect. You can only achieve this through experimenting.

Besides motivating your day, one of the main objectives of a high-performance morning routine is ensuring you register wins as early in the day as possible, no matter how small the victories may seem.

Why is this important? When you accomplish tasks immediately after waking up, your body produces dopamine—the neurotransmitter responsible for the 'feel-good feeling.' However, if your dopamine levels are low, it can lead to some of the following complications:

- Loss of satisfaction or pleasure

- Depression

- Compulsions

- Reduced levels of concentration and focus

- Lack of motivation

- Addictions and cravings

Now, this is not the best way to begin your day.

Strategies for Developing a High-Performance Morning Routine

An effective morning routine sets the pace for your day and is not only about morning rituals and a healthy breakfast but a collection of healthy and positive habits.

You can utilize numerous approaches to create a routine that suits the available time at your disposal in the morning and the goals you intend to achieve.

Here are a few timeless steps that can guide you on how to go about it:

Step 1: Prepare a list of all your planned morning activities

Consider this step as more of a brainstorming session. List all the activities that you wish to accomplish every morning. No idea is too silly or impractical at this point.

As you proceed to the later stages, you will have the opportunity to refine and fine-tune your list to remain with only the activities that are meaningful, practical, and value-adding.

Step 2: Arrange your tasks according to importance (ascending order)

Take time to determine which morning tasks are more important and place them on your list. This way, knowing where to put each task in your itinerary becomes easier.

Step 3: Tabulate your tasks

Tabulating your wish list enables you to determine important activities, those that are moderately essential, and those that are of less importance.

Step 4: Indicate the time it takes to complete each task

To enable prudent time management, this is a crucial activity. Try to be as precise as possible to ensure the time at your disposal in the morning supports your to-do list. For example, if you plan to include a quick workout, indicate how long it should take—the same applies to preparing a healthy breakfast.

Step 5: Place your list of activities in your calendar

At this point, you have already prioritized your tasks and listed them in order of importance. Now place them in your daily calendar as a reminder because nobody can remember everything. You can use a regular physical calendar or opt for tools such as AirTable or Google Calendar.

Step 6: Ensure consistency

Now that your morning routine is in place, it is time to swing into action. Ensure you take it every day, especially in the initial stages because getting back on track will require double the effort.

To ensure your morning routine is a success right from the onset, do not forget the following three crucial principles that we covered earlier:

- Prepare for your next day the night prior

- Begin your day with one or two simple tasks to activate your motivation—like making your bed

- Reserve the most difficult tasks for when you are at your sharpest and more focused, as opposed to later in the day when you are physically and mentally exhausted

The Miracle Morning Routine

One of the most effective, high-performance, tried-and-tested morning routines ever suggested is the *'Miracle Morning routine'* designed by life coach and best-selling author, Hal Elrod.

The Miracle Morning routine is a set of six activities dubbed *'life savers,'* with the ability to change your life and create time for tasks that enable you to boost your productivity and improve your overall quality of life. The Miracle Morning routine encourages you to wake up early, and you can complete all the suggested activities before 8 am.

The routine can apply to a wide range of activities and uses a highly flexible model that allows you to customize it to include activities that work for you.

Morning Miracle Overview

The best lessons come from personal experiences, and this effective routine is no different.

After a horrific accident that left him in a coma for almost a week, during which his girlfriend deserted him, and having to face bankruptcy shortly after and fighting depression, Elrod was in search of a way to change his life for the better. That is how the morning miracle or magic morning routine came to be.

Elrod said, *"I wanted to change, but I didn't know where to start. So I became interested in what successful people have in common. I came across something I didn't want to believe; they're all early risers. If I wanted to get out of my situation and have a better life, I had to get up early! That's where Miracle Morning was born and its simple principle: Get up early to do something positive."*

The main idea is to get up with a positive attitude every morning, quit feeling sorry for yourself no matter what you are going through, and do not settle for mediocrity. You also need to set realistic goals, obtain the right tools to achieve them, and allow your potential to surprise yourself and surpass your dreams.

Some of the benefits the magic morning routine promises include, but are not limited to:

- Waking up every morning in a structured way with more drive and energy to face the day

- Identify and embark on your life's purpose

- Lower your stress levels

- Improve your financial status

- Overcome life's challenges

- Show more gratitude and less worry

- Improve your overall health

- Boost your focus and productivity

Although it requires dedication and commitment, the magic morning routine is designed as a 30-day challenge to transform your morning ritual into an ingrained habit and a permanent feature in your life.

Steps and Activities Involved

Earlier, we mentioned the life savers routine, the activities that form the basis of this life-changing morning routine. **SAVERS** is an acronym for the tasks your high-performance exercise should involve:

- **S**ilence

- **A**ffirmations

- **V**isualization

- **E**xercise

- **R**eading

- **S**cribing

You can integrate any tasks that conform to each of the above stages. The main objective is to include activities that develop one or more of your spiritual, intellectual, physical, and emotional attributes.

Silence

This involves creating and finding the strength of serenity within yourself, and the idea is to begin your day on a soothing, calm, and positive note.

A moment of silence in the morning to reflect on your day ahead or express gratitude makes you appreciate the power of calmness around you. Additionally, silence reduces stress and morning anxiety and improves your ability to think and react accordingly to arising challenges.

Activities that promote silence may include breathing exercises, prayer or meditation, and mindfulness.

Affirmations

The set of activities that fall under affirmations harnesses the power of autosuggestion. Autosuggestion is where you repeat positive things to yourself to boost your psyche. The practice can positively impact your morale and well-being and play a central role in your success.

To achieve this, jot down a few positive personal statements about your life and read them aloud. This serves two purposes—to eliminate negative thoughts from your mind that may act as a hurdle to progress, and to reprogram your brain to lean more towards positive reviews.

Create affirmations that cover all aspects of your life, from family, friends, career objectives, financial targets, and social life to projects you may be undertaking currently or in the future.

In a nutshell, imagining and proclaiming yourself as the person you have always aspired to be helps you to become that person. Also, by believing in yourself and your abilities, you boost your chances of becoming that kind of person.

Visualization

By visualizing successful scenarios you wish to achieve down to the minutest detail, you tend to project yourself as a winner. Consequently, you perceive your goals as achievable and within your grasp.

Take at least five minutes every morning to visualize going through your perfect day, conducting your planned schedule without any hurdles but with ease, confidence, and great pleasure.

A positive vision is equivalent to the law of attraction—it reinforces your ability to believe in and access your vision.

Award-winning actor, Jim Carrey's story is a fitting example of how powerful visualization is. In

1987, before he made it big, he wrote himself a $10 million check bearing an end date of Thanksgiving Day 1995 for 'acting services rendered.' For years, he visualized his big payday; it finally arrived in 1994, one year earlier than he had envisioned when he landed a lead role in the movie, 'Dumb and Dumber.'

Exercise

An early morning workout—whether participating in a sport you love or simple physical exercise—can improve your emotional well-being and health. It can also increase your energy levels and improve the quality of your sleep, among numerous other benefits that traverse all aspects of your life. Activities such as swimming, jogging, running, gymnastics, or weightlifting can add immense value to your life.

Suppose you have a mobility or physical condition that does not allow you to engage in a regular exercise regimen. In that case, options such as yoga or basic stretch workouts can be sufficient. But remember that it is always wise to get the green light from your doctor before embarking on any exercise routine.

Reading

Be a voracious reader, and do it mainly for pleasure. Attempt reading at least a chapter or ten pages of a book that adds meaning to your life. By doing so, you will combine a fun way to learn new stuff with the benefits of entertainment.

While fiction is a great way to unwind, save fictional books for your evening. For your morning routine, strive to learn something new—self-help books fit this description perfectly. If you find a book has a positive impact, there is no harm in rereading it as many times as you like.

Scribing

Putting pen to paper and writing down your ideas is a great way to sort out and structure your thinking. The central concept of scribing is to keep a regular and updated journal—on paper or digitally, in line with your preferences. Your journal should record your positive thoughts and your goal achievement strategies and capture lessons learned or memorable moments, among several other possibilities.

Keeping a journal comes with a host of benefits, which include:

- It provides clarity on your goals and helps you remember your objectives.

- Photos, drawings, and illustrations let you visualize your positive thoughts.

- It allows you to trace your journey from where you started and establish your current status and destiny. This is also an effective method to keep track of your progress and identify what you need to do to achieve your goals.

- There is no restriction on the type of ideas you can pen—your journal can be home to your craziest thoughts alongside your wildest imaginations.

- A journal can be the source of or provide vital guidelines for your affirmations.

Assuming you have dedicated one hour to your morning routine, here is a suggestion on how you can schedule your time to reap maximum benefits:

- Silence – 5 minutes

- Affirmations – 5 minutes

- Visualization – 5 minutes

- Exercise – 20 minutes

- Reading – 20 minutes

- Scribing – 5 minutes

As mentioned earlier, this flexible routine should act as a benchmark that helps you create a customized morning ritual that caters to your unique and specific needs.

"If it's your job to eat a frog, it's best to do it first thing in the morning. And If it's your job to eat two frogs, it's best to eat the biggest one first."

— Mark Twain

Chapter 8

The Early Morning Habit Stack

"Believe that your day will be good and leave it up to your day to prove you wrong."

— Todd Stoker

In the initial days of implementing your morning routine, you may find that it is not a walk in the park. That is a regular occurrence that you should anticipate. As mentioned earlier, change is never easy, and neither is it handed on a silver platter. If you have the winning mentality of 'expect the worst but hope for the best,' you will soon realize how helpful it can be.

Think of all the things that can go wrong—you oversleep and don't hear the alarm, then you can't find your keys, discover the clothes you prepared the night before are full of fur as your cat slept on them, and to cap it all, you forget one of the essential tasks of the morning.

However, this can be different. A morning routine is one of the best ways to develop good habits. Your morning ritual should not be a horrific experience, even at the onset, once you understand the power of habit stacking.

What is Habit Stacking?

In Steve Scott's book, *'Habit Stacking: 97 Small Life Changes That Take Five Minutes or Less,'* he describes habit stacking as *"The essence of habit stacking is to take a series of small changes (like eating that piece of fruit) and build a ritual you follow daily."*

In our contemporary culture, where a large majority perceive 'bigger as better' and pursue significant breakthroughs, it is difficult to fathom that small, step-by-step changes can bring about exceptional results. But the truth is that it is possible because small changes inspire wins that provide much-needed encouragement, especially when we are on the brink of quitting.

But how can you build a morning routine you can religiously follow daily? You can use an existing, tried, and proven method of using a current habit to act as the trigger.

At the center of every habit is a primary neurological loop called the **habit loop**, which comprises three main parts.

The first part, the cue, instructs your brain to switch into automatic mode and identifies the exact habit to use. Interestingly, the most stable alerts occur immediately before your actions and mainly consist of behaviors you regularly perform.

Here is a probable example of an existing habit—a behavior you go through daily. But what exactly do you do immediately after?

On weekdays, you wake up and turn on your coffee machine. While the coffee brews, you jot down three items you are grateful for and your top five essential tasks of the day. You pour yourself a cup of coffee, open Google Drive, and begin the most important activity of your day.

You will notice from the above example that the trigger of every action is the completion of the habit that precedes it. We call this the Habit Staircase. It is usually difficult to wake up and dive straight into your morning routine, but it becomes easier once you build momentum through a series of small, simple steps.

The higher you go up the staircase, the more momentum you gain and the less motivation you require to complete your planned routine.

So, how can you implement this in your morning routine?

Morning Routine and Habit Stacking

When you set out to create your morning routine, begin by choosing the habit you want. Next, use an implementation intention. This involves identifying a pattern you will use as the trigger for your new intended habit. Use the following sequence and fill in the 'habit' blank.

After I (existing habit), I will (new pattern).

Here is a practical example:

- **After I wake up**, I will meditate and say three things I'm grateful for.

- After I switch on the coffee machine, I will perform ten push-ups.

- **After I put on my contact lenses**, I will read one chapter of a self-help book.

Please write down your implementation intention and place it somewhere it is visible every morning. Consider the list as instructions for your morning routine. If you do not commit, you may easily be distracted by anything.

Habit stacking is one of the best ways to develop your morning routine because it depends on another habit as a cue instead of a time or location. Going back to the example above, if your implementation intention reads something like this:

- After I wake up at 6.30 am, I will meditate and say three things I'm grateful for.

- After I switch on my coffee machine at 7 am, I will perform ten pushups.

- After I put on my contact lenses at 7.45 am, I will read one chapter of a self-help book.

What if you oversleep and wake up at 7.30 am? It will throw your entire morning routine into disarray, and you will probably not manage a single ritual. So many variables can mess up your morning routine if you peg it to exact times. On the other hand, when it depends on another habit, it becomes more flexible and versatile, and you will have a smooth time maintaining your morning routine, no matter what happens.

For example, if you oversleep and wake up at 7.30 am instead of 6.30 am, you can still manage to meditate, make your coffee, do your ten pushups, call an Uber or take the bus to work (instead of driving), and read a chapter of a self-help book on your way to work. You will notice that you will only need to make a minor adjustment or sacrifice, and your morning routine will remain on track despite waking up late.

In case your pushups, for instance, were pegged on switching on your coffee machine and you stopped taking coffee, find another habit (existing or new) to replace the habit you dropped to ensure continuity.

A fixed way to develop an effective morning routine needs to be in place. It all depends on what works best for you. However, the governing principle should be this:

If you wish to change your morning ritual, gradually switch one thing at a time instead of carrying out a complete overhaul. After all, it is the little hinges that swing big doors.

Pick one habit you wish to include in your routine, ensure it is super simple, and then make it automatic by performing it daily. Repeat this cycle to the point that you have a string of habits that you conduct spontaneously.

"Whether the day is for writing, designing, or painting, the consistent practice of a morning routine is the doorway into it all."

— Elle Luna

Chapter 9

Obstacles: Your Family, Work, Distractions, and Everything Else

"My routine serves as the building blocks for a successful day. It's a tool. I try not to get bogged down if I can't do it at all."

— Carly Stein

A morning routine comes with its share of obstacles that we can divide into two categories—internal and external—which can threaten to derail your newfound positive habits. Internal barriers mainly involve you, while external hurdles can range from family and friends to emerging issues you may not see coming.

While you should not expect smooth sailing in your quest to practice your morning routine, the good news is that there is always an at-hand solution to ensure your morning routine stays on track and remains true to its objective.

Weekday mornings are primed for failure. There always needs to be more time, your morning routine may depend on other household members, and there is always the possibility of something unexpected happening, ranging from sleeping through your alarm and uncooperative kids to the coffee machine breaking down.

Since a morning routine requires consistency and has a direct bearing on your day ahead, it is essential to know how to maneuver around, go over, or under any obstacles—because the show must go on, after all.

Here are some of the most common hurdles that can be temporary setbacks and how you can tackle them to avoid messing up your morning routine and day:

Never Enough Time

If your morning and routine feel like one mad rush against time, and you are always playing catch up, it may be time to take a hard look at your performance and make the necessary adjustments. It is unhealthy if basic activities are all you have time for in the morning. To establish where the problem lies, ask yourself the following questions:

Am I waking up early enough?

Depending on when you leave the house for work, you need to wake up at least two hours before your departure time to enable a successful morning routine. For example, if you leave the house at 8 am, your wake-up time should be at least 6 am. This ensures you have ample time to complete your planned tasks comfortably.

However, this also depends on the activities you intend to perform as part of your morning routine. The longer your to-do list is, the more time you require and the earlier you need to wake up.

Am I biting off more than I can chew?

It is practically impossible to have a morning routine to-do list that takes two hours to complete if you only have an hour for the tasks. Try to prioritize the items on your to-do list and stick to the most important—only the things that contribute to your goals of the day and your long-term goals.

If anything on your list does not meet this criterion, weed it out, or allocate it another time, such as in your evening routine. If you consider everything in your long to-do list necessary, you can adjust your wake-up time to accommodate all your planned morning activities or carry out some of them the night before.

Also, be realistic. If you make an unrealistic schedule of activities for your morning routine, you are setting yourself up to fail.

Does my wake-up time allow 7-9 hours of slumber?

For the umpteenth time, a healthy adult requires 7-9 hours of sleep every night, and the time you sleep every night must factor in this crucial aspect. This could also be why you need more time to perform your entire morning routine—you use up your sleep on other activities, especially in the evening.

Therefore, create a sleep time that supports the recommended hours of sleep—and strictly adhere to it. Doing this will ensure your morning routine can pan out as planned without feeling pressed for time.

Do I enjoy conducting the activities on my to-do list?

Your morning routine should be created by you and for you. If you are waking up to tasks you do not enjoy or look forward to, you are asking too much of yourself and it is bound to be a tall order that will be difficult to sustain.

Maybe you have a passion for getting fit, but weightlifting is not your style. If you find a jog or a walk better, by all means, go for it. Or perhaps you are struggling to meditate... in that case, yoga could be a great substitute. Secondly, do not feel obligated to copy somebody else's morning routine. Choose what works best for you.

Family Hurdles

Family can either be an enabler or an obstacle to your morning routine.

If you have a family, your morning routine may be a collective activity, or you probably begin yours earlier, and the rest of the family joins in at some point. Imagine trying to have your five minutes of quiet mindfulness, meditation, or reading while the kids go for each other's jugular in the next room—at the top of their voices. It will prove to be an effort in futility.

However, no child wakes up in the morning thinking, 'This is the day I'm going to make my parents' day miserable.' But anyone can forgive you for having such ideas. Kids can be a handful in the morning. Getting them out of bed can be a nightmare, and it is not uncommon to wrestle them out of bed, together with their beddings, while yelling your head off. As if that is not enough, they may refuse to eat their breakfast or get upset over a trivial issue—like being unable to find their favorite shoes.

The solution to this scenario, familiar to many families in the morning, is psychological.

How often do your kids wake up to you by their bedside, gently persuading them to wake up? Or are they used to shouts of, "Get up! It's late!"

Although the suggested solution outlined below may take time, it is worth it in the end because it will allow your and the family's morning routine to flow smoothly:

- Be gentle while waking up the kids, and take a few minutes to talk about their expectations for the day. The idea is to create motivation for them to get up.

- Resolve activities like what to have for breakfast—which can take up much time—the night before, with all the ingredients prepared.

- Kids respond well to visual stimulation. Create a checklist of the activities your kids should carry out in the morning with their input. The list has to include tasks they enjoy doing.

- Attempt to connect with the kids instead of constantly trying to correct them. For example, you can listen to how complicated your kid's science project is or help them make breakfast. This allows you to offer support, play the role of a life coach, and connect with them.

If you live with your spouse, you can both create complimentary morning routines or one with activities you both enjoy to avoid clashing interests. Also, to keep both your motivation levels high, you can act as each other's accounting partners to ensure your morning routines are observed and sustained.

Career-Related Obstacles

According to studies, the two most common stressors among working adults originate from work and money issues. Stress from the two can lead to anxiety, irritability, and anger, which eventually leads to burnout or depression. That is why work-related activities should not feature in your morning routine.

Trying to complete or get ahead of a work-related assignment before you leave for work wastes valuable time you can utilize for a more meaningful activity while preventing you from achieving the elusive and coveted work-life balance.

When you begin your work day in the morning at home, it comes at a price because your objectives and goals suffer in the process.

Develop a habit of always leaving your job-related activities at your place of work, including devices you use in your work duties. If possible, have two phones—a personal gadget and one for work, and always leave the latter behind when you go home. Doing this will eliminate the temptation to answer work-related calls or take a peek at messages during your morning routine.

Internal Conflict

Like everything else, there is nothing like a 'perfect' morning routine. However, having a morning routine that gives you a feeling of security and control towards the start of your day is an essential part of your overall well-being.

However, it is always good to remember that without boundaries, your morning routine can quickly become obsessive behavior, limiting and trapping you daily. This often occurs when you fail to meet certain aspects of your morning ritual as well as you might have liked. This can quickly spiral into perceptions of low self-esteem and self-criticism.

If you are prone to anxiety, it is possible to get fixated on things that you may think make you feel better—when they do not. When this happens, you tend to develop a form of rigidity that can become obsessive and aggravate your anxiety.

For example, if working out features in your morning routine, and for one reason or another, you cannot exercise, your entire day can be full of anxiety, worry, and guilt. This can spiral out of control and become a fixation during the next morning's routine.

Additionally, that night, you may lose sleep over your failure to work out and begin worrying about how you will manage it the following morning to prevent a repeat.

Adhering to a strict morning routine could also be a sign of trying to be a perfectionist, which could be self-destructive, exhausting, and a dangerous way of thinking.

Routines that are too rigid tend to become jaded with time, draw resentment, and build low morale for the involved activities. Also, such a morning routine stifles creativity and motivation since it does not allow a new way of doing things.

Which begs the question, "So, if a perfect morning routine is unattainable, what is the solution?" The answer is simple—balance.

According to accredited counselor, Dee Johnson, *"Balance is all about finding the middle path—the world is not black or white. Use kind, respectful self-talk if you cannot always manage it. It's okay and part of being human. Successful thinking is about being flexible and building confidence as you learn to trust that you can make good and varied choices for yourself and that you are capable."*

Additionally, it is all about taking a good look at the activities you include in your morning routine. Establish your motivation and derive genuine pleasure from your tasks because forcing yourself to go through activities you do not enjoy for happiness or success will never achieve the desired results.

The best approach is to identify a perspective that mirrors who you are currently, supporting and celebrating this version of yourself instead of a projected future version. This is because the happiest people are those who enjoy what they do from day to day.

"These morning practices fuel me; keeping my routine is not about willpower."

– Jenny Blake

Conclusion: Morning Routines

"I think routines should flex and change. Mine feels like a dynamic, malleable thing that emerges organically rather than a rigid set of steps I must follow or plan for."

— *Kate Nafisi*

Anybody can adopt a morning routine. It does not matter what your current morning looks like. Whether you are not a morning person or a bubbly early riser, there is a morning routine that will complement and support your day ahead and your overall goals in life.

Instead of life seeming to be on top of you, a morning routine places the control of your life exclusively in your hands—and you end up on top. Besides the power it offers, a morning routine also provides unlimited flexibility.

For example, life can sometimes get in the way and result in a misstep or something unexpected, like the pandemic. With a morning routine, you can work around whatever life deals you, make a few adjustments here and there, and modify your morning routine to adapt to any changes that may emerge.

This means that once you begin your morning routine, it is possible to sustain it to infinity—it is a sustainable model and approach that is not easy to disrupt unless you allow it. Not many aspects of life come with such a level of guarantee and security.

The set structure that makes a morning routine can eliminate distractions and the scattered thoughts that tend to build into stress or feeling overwhelmed.

As a result, a dedicated morning ritual enables you to be more aware of time and efficient while also taking off any pressures in your life and those of others. Research also shows that a morning routine can benefit people with insomnia, ADHD, and bipolar disorder.

All these benefits that can positively transform your life are yours. But first, you need to take that leap of faith and begin crafting a morning routine full of activities you enjoy that can add that missing spark to your life.

Secondly, your proposed to-do list should also contain activities that align with your kind of day and overall goals—like Woody Allen aptly stated, *"Eighty percent of success is showing up."*

A morning routine enables you to show up for your morning, day, dreams, and aspirations, and improve your general quality of life.

You've got this. Now, wake up, get up, and make it happen!

Scott Allan

"I don't recommend my routine, but I do recommend evaluating your routine and developing one that supports the things you love the most."

*— **George Foreman III***

About Scott Allan

Scott Allan is an international bestselling author of 25+ books published in over 12 languages in the area of personal growth and self-development. He is the author of **Fail Big**, **Undefeated,** and **Do the Hard Things First**.

As a former corporate business trainer in Japan, and **Transformational Mindset Strategist**, Scott has invested over 10,000 hours of research and instructional coaching into the areas of self-mastery and leadership training.

With an unrelenting passion for teaching, building critical life skills, and inspiring people around the world to take charge of their lives, Scott Allan is committed to a path of **constant and never-ending self-improvement**.

Many of the success strategies and self-empowerment material that is reinventing lives around the world evolves from Scott Allan's 20 years of practice and teaching critical skills to corporate executives, individuals, and business owners.

You can connect with Scott at:

scottallan@scottallanpublishing.com

Empower Your Thoughts (Bonus Chapter #1)

Turn the page to read a chapter from **Empower Your Thoughts** (Book #2 in the *Pathways to Mastery* series)

Reduce Your Worry Habit

If you observe your own thinking and how your mind interacts with the world, you become a passenger on a wild ride through a theme park. You can be a witness to all the noise and mayhem that comes with a polluted mind that won't stay in the moment.

People are constantly dealing with their thoughts that focus on "getting" and "having" and "becoming." We are attached to owning something or attached to becoming something.

When things are not going as planned, your mind flips into worry mode. Worry is always grounded in the fear of the future. Worrisome thoughts are thoughts we give permission to take control of our state of mind. We worry when we lack trust or faith.

If faith is the belief that things will work out, worry is the belief that everything is in danger of falling apart. It won't work out. You could fail. This could happen or that could happen. Your thoughts start to play out the worst-case scenarios of a bad outcome that results in you ending up empty handed, broke, or alone.

Worry is a broken loop of fear. This is a daily struggle with the mind. You want to trust in something bigger than yourself, but you can't. So, how can you fight back against the loop of fear that worry creates? How do you stop worrying about the future "possibilities" and start living?

You'll need to bring yourself back to the present moment. It starts with reframing your situation and life in a positive framework. Are you seeing the world as a scary, frightful place? Are you afraid of waking up and finding yourself homeless one day? Do you think you'll lose your job next week?

Well, all these things could happen—or none of them could happen. The extent to which they happen is up to you. Most of the worst things that will ever happen to you take place in your mind first... and that's it! Think about the grand symphony of chaos that is constantly conducted inside your mind. But you, as the conductor of your thoughts, can choose how and what to think about. Imagine that. You are the master of your own mind. Remind yourself of this fact and take time to observe your thoughts.

We always have ideas, voices and opinions, mixed with conflicting thoughts based on information we are not entirely sure is correct. How do you separate the good from the bad? How can you trust what is real and what is misleading? How do you stay mindful when your mind wants to wander, explore, and create its own reality without permission?

The strategy I use to filter out the thoughts I don't need is a mental discipline that gets you to focus in on just the present moment. As most of your thoughts jump around and can be in the past one minute and the present the next, this form of mental conditioning—also known as **reframing your thinking portal**—works because it turns down the volume on noisy, intrusive thoughts.

Worry is conditioning your thoughts to fear. If you were raised by fearful parents, and spent most of your youth surrounded by fearful people, then being a worrier will seem the best course of action. This way, you build up your fears of the future and don't take any action for fear of failing.

Right now, make a list of three areas of your life you consistently worry about. Knowing what your triggers are plays a big part in this. Then, when you think about these areas, what thoughts enter your mind? Common themes are thoughts of scarcity, losing something valuable, failing fast, or being embarrassed if your master plan doesn't work out.

You might have fearful thoughts of money or relationships, worry about losing your job or getting ill. These are all legitimate worries. But worry leads to mental paralysis by default, and without taking positive action, you'll end up doing nothing. This ensures the worry habit sticks with its rotation and sets up a loop to capture your thoughts. You must unravel that loop and dismantle the worry habit.

You can empower your thoughts by feeding empowering messages to your mind. It works like the body. If you eat crap and junk food, you're going to feel like a physical garbage can. The mind is no different. Worrisome thoughts generate anxiety. You only get out of it what you feed into it.

Here is how you can eliminate the worry habit right now and gain control over the triggers that set you off.

Worry Thoughts are Fabrications

Worry is believing in false stories that have not come true. You worry about having no money, and yet, there is no evidence to suggest you will always be broke. Maybe you worry about your health and that you might get sick. Well, you will not be healthy forever, you know that. But you have your health today, don't you? Worrisome thoughts are grounded in future fear, like most things we stress about.

Worry is another form of fear. We create most of our fears. They play out in our minds and take over all common sense. What are you worrying about right now? Is it something now or something supposed to happen later?

When you feed into the worry habit, you reinforce the false stories that will likely never happen.

From now on, feed your mind the good stuff it really wants. Try these affirmations instead:

- "I am not worried about tomorrow because today is perfect. The here and now is what I have."

- "I always worry about losing my job, but this has never happened to me. I am a good employee and the company I work for values its workers. Why would I think it could happen now?"

Break down your worrisome thoughts and expose these demons for what they are: False fabrications that rarely happen. Worry is a habit, and you can break any habit. But you can make your worrisome beliefs come true, too. If you believe that you will be broke, lose your health, or get divorced, then by carrying this worry around with you can manifest it to come true.

Remember: Thoughts have power and can draw toward you the bad as well as the good. If you think you're going to lose your job, you might show up at work acting like someone who doesn't deserve to be there.

Do you think your spouse is going to divorce you? This worry could cause you to become paranoid. Soon you start to track his or her whereabouts until they catch you planting a GPS unit underneath the car. So, while worrisome thinking is grounded in fantasy, you can manifest your worst nightmares to happen by holding onto these worrisome thoughts.

Negative Thinking: Hardwired for Fear

Positive thinking only works if you truly believe the message you're sending to your brain.

There are a few things I want to say about negative thinking. We tend to see negative thinking as something bad that you should be ashamed of. I'll admit that thinking positively and acting in a positive manner is much better than doing things in a negative way. But, it's a philosophy of mine that negative energy is just as important as positive energy.

How can that be?

You must walk through a mile of slimy mud sometimes before you can get to the green grass on the other end. In other words, being negative and experiencing the suffering that goes with it can be a great motivator for making the decision to change.

Negative thinking—or, "living a negative lifestyle", as I like to call it—is a sign that something is not right with your life. Believe it or not, some people seem to enjoy the attention they receive from negative thinking.

If you have an NMA (i.e., Negative Mental Attitude), and you are not happy with this, deciding to switch over to a positive frame of mind requires that you take intentional action to get your momentum moving.

Some of the world's greatest success stories have come from people who lived through hell and decided to change their lives. You can also look at the people who have everything going for them, and yet, they are unhappy, and it shows in their attitude.

I truly believe that living a positive lifestyle has very little to do with how much you own or how successful you are. It comes down to attitude in every aspect of your life. If all it took was money and popularity, then there wouldn't be any misery with people who seemingly have everything.

Thought and Circumstances: How to Attract What You Want

If you are unhappy with your present circumstances, whether it be your job, relationships, or current state of mind, there is only one way to change it: Think differently. I know this sounds like an obvious piece of advice, but there are reasons for this.

Do you know what happens when you think differently? Things on the outside begin to change.

Your situation can only change if you do. Here is why.

Your outer world will always reflect the inner. Your success or failure is based on the success and failure going on inside. Succeed in programming your thoughts for having positive experiences and that is what will happen.

People have been known to alter the course of their lives with a shift in attitude. Can you imagine where you would be if you focused everything you had on thinking with a positive attitude? This isn't to say thinking alone will change you, but without it, we can't follow up with positive actions.

What exactly are positive actions? Some examples are: helping people, working toward goals that get you unstuck, streamlining your efforts to make life worth living for yourself and those around.

The circumstances of this life do not control you. While we can't always choose our circumstances, we can decide how to view them. It is just a matter of fact that bad things happen. Life doesn't go according to plan, and it isn't always fun—no matter who you are or how positive your thoughts may be. But you can train yourself in the best way to deal with it.

Empower Your Focus
(Bonus Chapter #2)

Turn the page to read a chapter from **Empower Your Focus** (Book #4 in the *Pathways to Mastery* series)

The Process of Building Focus

You've understood what focus truly is, why it matters, and how to channel the different forms of focus to your advantage. But how do you go about building focus? Where do you begin? What process do you follow, and how do you ensure your pursuit of building focus is not only fruitful but, is also sustainable and enjoyable?

The key is to begin with one thing to focus on, to complete this task or meet this goal, and then move on to your next pursuit, thus creating a continuous flow of victories, each one fueling the next. Success begets success, and the more wins you rack up, the greater confidence you will develop in your deep focus sessions.

Focus on One Thing Until Done

We've found ourselves in a world where multi-tasking is the norm and focusing on one thing at a time is an exception. However, in doing so, we sacrifice the potential for our brains to level up and cultivate the right mind with the best training.

Conditioning the mind to focus on and accomplish task after task, goal after goal, with the help of the right habits, delivers the outcome you truly desire. Instead of ending up with whatever cheap pleasure that's derived from instant gratification, you reap the benefits of a focused mind trained to execute on priority tasks.

The more we repeatedly do something, the easier it becomes to do; it becomes a pattern, a *good habit*. The scientific term for this practice is 'automaticity'. It's the ability of your mind to let you do something on autopilot. It takes a great deal of effort and time to set up a new habit.

While some studies claim it takes 21 days, others state it takes 66 days and some even say it takes 254 days for a new habit to be fully ingrained in you - but once you've managed to establish a new habit, your activity will be almost automatic. When you focus on one thing only, and one thing after another at a time, each one becomes easier to do as it becomes habitual.

Here are a few techniques which will set you on the path to building focus and sharpening your mind.

Technique 1: Create goals for yourself

It is said that the difference between a dream and a goal is that a dream is a gift you *wish to receive*, whereas a goal is an outcome you *work to achieve*. Without a concrete goal, you can't have a clear plan. Without a plan, your actions will have no particular direction, and your energies will be expended wastefully.

Here are 11 steps to help you identify, articulate, and clearly define your goals:

1. Begin with an idea dump. List out all the things you've wanted to achieve, without setting any limitations in your mind.

2. Choose your master goal. What is it that you want the most in your life? Don't winnow it down — be bold in what you're asking of yourself, and trust that you will figure out a way to make it happen. Once you've chosen your master goal, write it down and commit to it.

3. Put a timeline to your goal. It doesn't matter if it is 2 months, 2 years, or 20 years — but put a definite timeline.

4. Break down your big goal. What will you need to accomplish in the next 1 year? Reverse engineer your big goal by writing down all the steps necessary to achieve it (hence, the next step).

5. Break your big goal down into 'sub-goals'. Make a list of every task, no matter how small, and identify what it is and how much time required to finish it. Think of this as your to-do list — what simple tasks will help you move towards accomplishing your goal?

6. Prioritize your action steps. What do you need to do right away, and what's not as urgent?

7. Visualize your success daily. Feeling how you would feel once you've accomplished your goal will fuel you to work towards it.

8. Become part of a supportive community. Invite accountability into your lifestyle. You don't have to do everything all by yourself!

9. Be mindful of your obstacles. Are you missing key resources? Do you hold limiting beliefs that are sabotaging you in your quest? Be honest and list out your obstacles so that you can find ways to overcome them.

10. Identify the skills and knowledge you need to reach your goal.

11. Continuously and honestly review your progress. Set up weekly and monthly review sessions to get an accurate benchmark of your progress.

Follow these steps and you should be well on your way to building an extraordinary level of focus.

Technique 2: Build 'focus blocks' to improve productivity

Using 'focus blocks' refers to chalking out chunks of time on your calendar for specific activities. Doing your taxes? Block out time on your calendar. Brainstorming ideas for your next project? Set aside time. Whatever task is pressing, whether it be attending your child's concert or much-required me-time, you want to dedicate time exclusively to that activity for that particular period of time.

Scheduling time is the easy part – the harder part is to ensure that you work only on that specific activity for that chunk of time, ignoring all else. This includes not checking up on interrupting emails and not pausing for a colleague dropping by for some quick help.

Here are **7 quick tips** to help you:

1. Commit to your scheduling system.

2. Use your calendar, use your stickies, use a daily planner - use every tool at your disposal to help you stick to your system.

3. Make a reasonable schedule – you don't want to burn out in the process of reaching for your optimum level of focus.

4. Get your colleagues onboard – you can share your calendar so that they can see when you're available.

5. Find a quiet and comfortable spot to work without distraction.

6. Work in sync with your natural cycle. When do you concentrate best? Set your schedule accordingly.

7. Don't give up. If you find yourself off course, gently bring yourself back to plan.

It's hard to get into the system of working with focus blocks. But, once you commit to it—and discuss it with your colleagues—you can request that they not interrupt, and you'll find a tremendous boost in productivity.

Technique 3: Use focus-building activities in a group setting

While the first two techniques were inward-focused, here's another technique to help you start building better focus, and this one can be group-based. Pick a focus-building activity, and schedule time with friends or family centered around this activity. Think 'puzzle-night'!

You probably worked on a lot of puzzles as a child –puzzles are a great way to stimulate the mind and build focus not only in children, but also in adults.

Here are **five benefits** of using puzzles as a work-out for your brain:

1. Improve cognitive function and spatial reasoning

2. Develop better attention to detail

3. Improve your memory, especially short-term memory

4. Enhance your problem-solving ability and IQ over time

5. Immerse yourself in an esteem-boosting activity and reduce stress

If jigsaw puzzles aren't your thing, you can go with crossword games, solve brain teasers, work with Sudoku, or even use apps such as Luminosity. If you're a chess player, it can be a fantastic way improve focus as well.

No matter which technique you choose to begin your journey of improving your ability to focus, you want to ensure you commit to one thing at a time and stay on course.

The process of building focus is an ongoing challenge, but it comes with life-changing rewards that make it totally worth the commitment.

Pathways to Mastery Series

Master Your Life One Book at a Time

Available where eBooks, books and audiobooks are sold.

Scott Allan

"Master Your Life One Book at a Time."

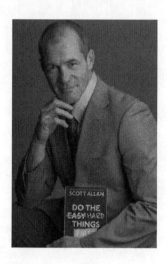

<u>Subscribe</u> to the weekly newsletter for actionable content and updates on future book releases from Scott Allan.

Made in the USA
Columbia, SC
03 November 2023

25444426R00093